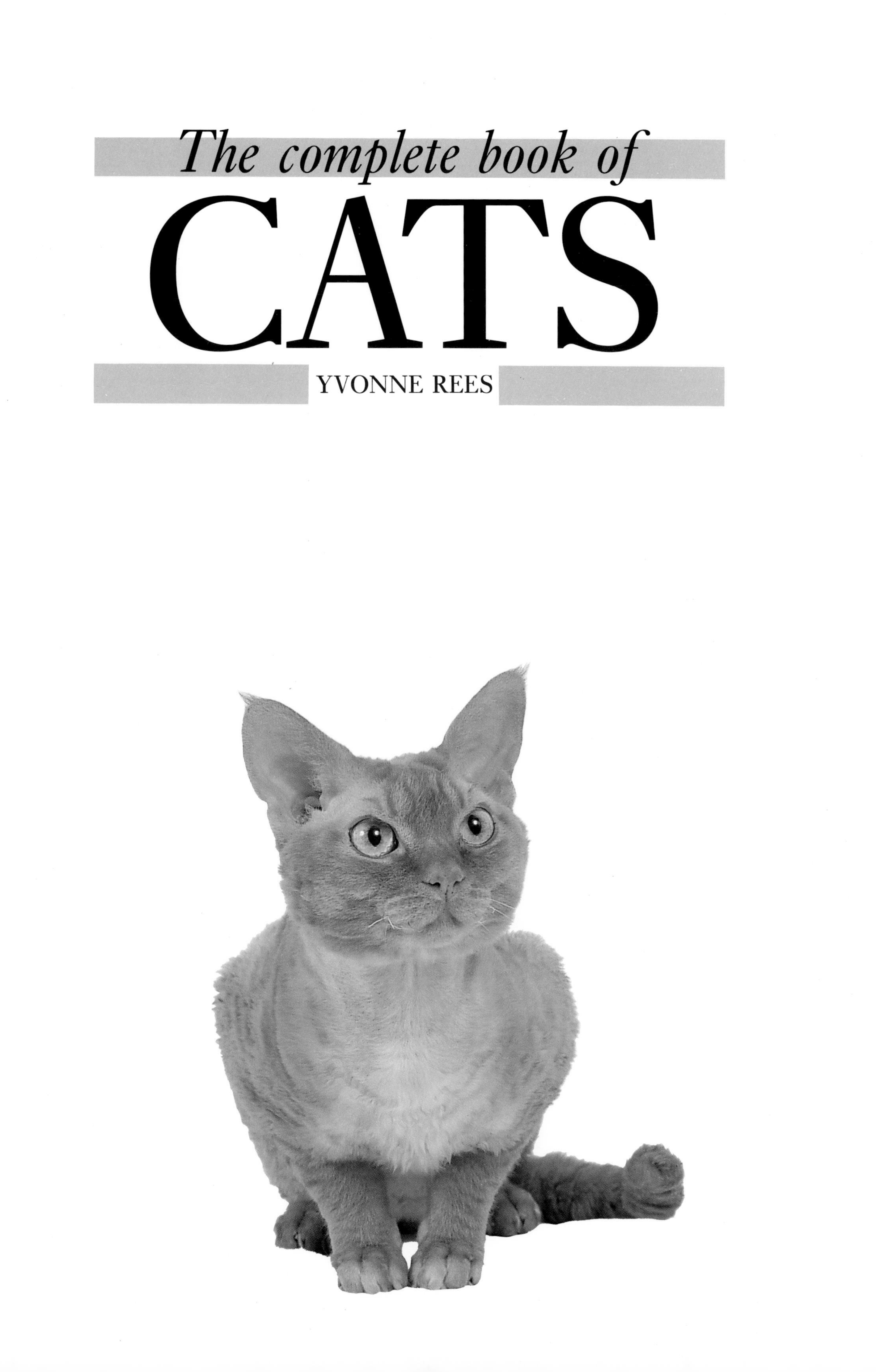

The complete book of

CATS

YVONNE REES

The complete book of CATS

YVONNE REES

CRESCENT BOOKS
NEW YORK • AVENEL, NEW JERSEY

CLB 2755

This 1993 edition published by Crescent Books,
distributed by Outlet Book Company, Inc.,
a Random House Company
40 Engelhard Avenue, Avenel, New Jersey 07001
Printed and bound in Hong Kong.

ISBN 0 517 06593 2
8 7 6 5 4 3 2 1

The Author
Yvonne Rees is a writer and lecturer on a wide range of subjects, including wildlife and animals. She shares her home in the country with a variety of domestic animals (and many wild ones), including two cats and two dogs. Looking after pets for friends and neighbors has involved Yvonne in keeping an eye on anything from quails and peacocks to cats, dogs, goats, hens and sheep. In her spare time she likes to paint, and has often turned her hand to preparing pet portraits for proud owners.

Credits
Edited and designed: Ideas into Print, Vera Rogers and Stuart Watkinson
Photographs: Marc Henrie, C. M. Dixon, David Keith Jones
Layouts: Sue Cook Typesetting: Ideas into Print
Commissioning Editor: Andrew Preston
Production: Ruth Arthur, Sally Connolly, Andrew Whitelaw
Director of Production: Gerald Hughes
Color Separations: Advance Laser Graphic Arts (International) Ltd., Hong Kong.

Above: *A pet tabby kitten looking for adventure in the garden. It is important that a young cat grows up to be confident and unafraid and so it should be introduced to all aspects of everyday life during the first four or five months of its life.*

Endpapers: *A splendid Blue-point Birman surveys the world from its favorite spot in the rockery.*

Half-title page: *A Silver Red Devon Rex poses patiently for the camera, its brittle curly whiskers typically broken off at the ends.*

Title page: *A Blue-point Siamese shows off its handsome coloring, its characteristically vivid blue eyes and the elegant profile of its body.*

Contents

The cat in history

As it stalks a ball of silver paper across the kitchen floor or pounces on a hapless shrew in the garden, your cat is no doubt totally unaware that its instinctive hunting skills are in part inherited from that fierce and probably best-known Ice Age beast pictured in the history books, the saber-toothed tiger. By the time the saber-tooth, with its improbable fangs, had died out - about three million years ago - the cat family had become sleeker and more intelligent, already recognizable as the three groups we know today - the big cats, such as lions and tigers *(Panthera)*; cats with claws that do not retract, such as cheetahs *(Acinonyx)*; and the small cats (*Felis*) that resemble our domestic pets. Often, it is easy to see how domestic cats are the result of crossbreeding in the past between the wild cats of the world - the European wild cat (*Felis sylvestris*), the African wild cat (*Felis libyca*) and the lithe jungle cat (*Felis chaus*) - because their tabby markings are so close to the camouflage coats of their wilder cousins. All cat breeds are naturally striped or spotted; such tendencies are simply suppressed in the self-colored, (meaning single-colored) and other highly bred pedigrees. Archaeologists and paleontologists are still trying to piece together

***Above:** Although feral domestic cats sometimes interbreed with European and African wild cats to produce interesting hybrids, wild cats of different species cannot breed successfully and so their species type has remained true. The African wild cat* (Felis lybica) *shown here survives in a wide range of habitats except desert and tropical forest, and is believed to be the primary ancestor of today's domestic cat. It clearly resembles a tabby pet cat.*

***Below:** Of all the larger wild cats, the cheetah is given a genus of its own -* Acinonyx *- because its claws do not fully retract as they do in other cat species, including the domestic cat. The spotted coat provides effective camouflage.*

***Right:** Cats were so revered by the Ancient Egyptians that they were often mummified and laid in tombs and temples.*

the puzzle of the exact line of descent to the earliest domesticated breeds of Ancient Egypt and Rome and subsequently to the purebred pedigree in the show ring or kitten on the hearth. The cat has had a rather checkered career since it first came out of the jungle and attracted the attention of man. We know that the Egyptians kept domesticated cats as long ago as 3000BC to keep down the numbers of vermin, such as rats and mice. Later, their graceful and haughty natures encouraged the practice of cat worship and the deification of the cat goddess, Bast. As well as the thousands of mummified cats found in temples, caves and cat cemeteries, some simply wrapped in straw or linen, others in elaborate cat-shaped coffins, there is a wealth of bronze figures, statues and paintings showing the cat at work and worship. Most of the early civilizations attempted to domesticate cats, sometimes as a source of food, as in China, or to control rats and mice in the towns' growing food stores.

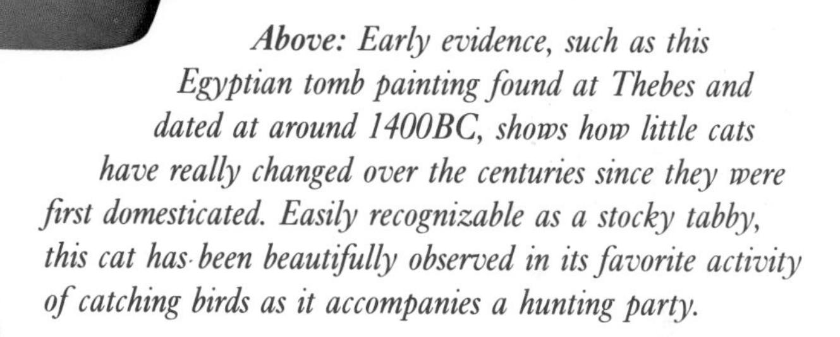

Above: Early evidence, such as this Egyptian tomb painting found at Thebes and dated at around 1400BC, shows how little cats have really changed over the centuries since they were first domesticated. Easily recognizable as a stocky tabby, this cat has been beautifully observed in its favorite activity of catching birds as it accompanies a hunting party.

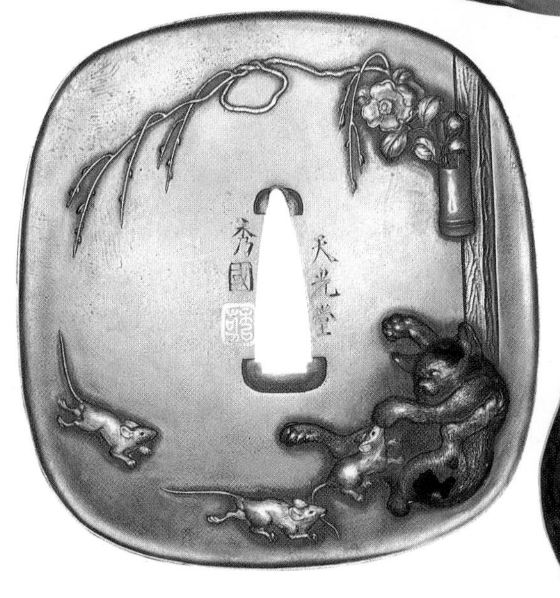

Above: Cats have always been valued for their skill in controlling vermin, as celebrated on this 19th-century Japanese shield guard. At one time, so many were kept for clearing homes and palaces of mice that few were left to patrol the city granaries and food stores.

Right: The black cat is traditionally believed to be the witch's assistant, helping her in her evil work, as depicted in this 19th-century pottery figurine from Pecs in Hungary. Many cats were destroyed through such superstition.

Later on, the activities of pioneering merchants and conquering armies resulted in a much greater movement of people, goods and also live animals between countries and continents. The Romans brought the domestic cat to Europe, where it interbred with local feral cats, producing a much stockier, broader type of animal than the slender foreign breed kept by the Egyptians. By the Middle Ages, the cat's position, in Europe at least, was far less favorable. Keen to the point of paranoia to stamp out paganism, the Christian Church persecuted cats and their owners in the name of devil worship and a great many cats were burnt alive. It was not until the eighteenth century that they regained their popularity as a harmless, even useful household pet. By the nineteenth century, they had again become, if not gods and goddesses, at least prized possessions: different breeds of cats began to be identified and the first cat shows were inaugurated.

Anatomy of a cat

The cat is superbly designed as a hunter. Even the most pampered show cat is fully equipped to survive in the wild, and the longhaired breeds that need so much grooming would molt on a seasonal basis, revealing a much slimmer, sleeker profile in the summer months. The cat's body shape and skeleton are perfectly adapted to allow it to move at speed, and anyone who has observed a cat in motion can only admire its agility and grace. Powerful hindlegs and a flexible spine, combined with enviable muscle control and coordination, allow it to crouch, twist, run and leap with perfect balance. The small head and shoulders enable a cat to negotiate the smallest spaces, while the advantages offered by the retractable claws make running, climbing and catching prey all the more efficient. The senses of smell, hearing and sight are all highly developed too, enabling the cat to pick up the sound or movement of insects and small rodents, even in poor light conditions. The powerful jaws and sharp teeth are designed to deliver the final blow at first bite. Add to that a tongue that can serve both as a spoon for liquids and a rough brush for grooming, and it is not surprising that the cat has a reputation for being self-reliant. The smallest kitten reveals its ancient hunting instincts by stalking, pouncing and snarling. Every cat marks out its territory - and in a town or city that may only be the smallest square of a backyard or alley - and defends it fiercely against intruders, standing its ground, arching its back and fluffing out its fur to make itself look bigger. Baring the fangs, hissing and spitting are also designed to make the animal look more ferocious than perhaps it feels. Some of the cat's characteristics and instincts have become almost legendary, even exaggerated and misunderstood. For example, it is true that when a cat falls from a height it invariably lands on its feet - not through any magical powers, but thanks to an incredible self-righting ability whereby the spine and tail twist the body in a spiral of up to 180° so that the feet land first. Should the cat tumble only a short distance, it may well not have time for such gymnastics and falls more awkwardly. The belief that cats can see in the dark is also based half on myth, half on truth. In total darkness, cats cannot see any better than humans, but they do have increased sensitivity in dim light, an essential attribute for a night hunter. The reason why a cat's eyes seem to shine out when caught in a beam of light is the presence of the *tapetum lucidum* at the back of the retina, a layer of crystalline cells that acts like a mirror to reflect the slightest available light back through the retina and thus improve night vision. As well as being highly refined physically, the cat has a well-developed intelligence. It will learn to use a litter tray, scratching post and cat flap from a very early age and, if you have the patience and start when the cat is young enough, it will learn a range of tricks as impressive as any dog.

Above: *Arching its back and fluffing up the fur makes a cat appear bigger and more aggressive than it really is - a useful ploy when it is suddenly taken unawares or threatened.*

Left: *A lion baring its teeth is a clear reminder that its cousin the domestic cat is a true carnivore. Those sharp teeth are specially adapted to kill prey and cut cleanly through the flesh.*

Right: *The cat's natural instincts as a hunter remain strong even in the most cherished, domestic household pet. You will find they often like to seek out some lofty perch, such as a tree-top or roof, which offers an excellent vantage point from which they can survey their territory. A flexible back and strong hindleg muscles mean the cat is a good climber, leaping up and clinging with its hooked claws. However, this equipment isn't so efficient when attempting to climb downwards.*

Below: *If you think cats seem to be asleep a lot of the time – you'd be right. The average cat spends two thirds of its life asleep – which is about twice as much as any other animal. The warmer, more comfortable and better fed they are, the more they'll sleep. Some cats sleep because they are bored. Cats will sleep in short spells – catnapping as we call it – rather than spend one long stretch asleep. This may be a light nap in which the cat remains semi-alert, or a much deeper sleep where the body is more relaxed.*

Right: *Cats love to feel warm and will even move their position to follow the warmth of the sun or singe their fur in an attempt to get close to the fire. Every cat has its favorite sleeping place, one that may not always be convenient to the rest of the household. Your bed is often popular and if you prefer to discourage this practice – perhaps through reasons of hygiene – you will have to make sure doors and windows are securely fastened as cats can be remarkably determined and cunning in their search for a suitable spot.*

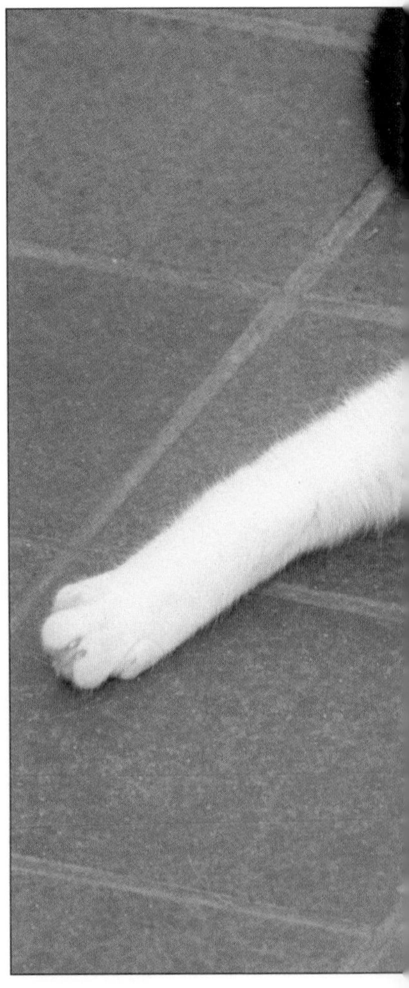

Right: *Cats use their tails for balance, rather in the way that a tightrope walker uses a long pole. Should the cat be walking along a narrow fence or wall and decide to look down in a certain direction, for example, it will automatically shift its center of gravity by moving its tail in the opposite direction as a counterbalance. A cat's eye-to-muscle and joint coordination is also extremely fast, which contributes further to its excellent sense of balance. Should a cat fall, it has the added advantage of a complex righting reflex that in the majority of cases ensures that it turns in the air to land safely on its feet. The only problem occurs where a cat falls a relatively short distance and does not have the time to right itself before landing.*

***Right:** The ears are highly sensitive, detecting the slightest sound with excellent accuracy. Their position is a good indication of mood too: held erect but pressed back slightly when angry or threatened; completely flattened down when frightened, as here.*

Left: ***Left:*** *A male Turkish Van cat spraying a strong-smelling urine to mark out its adopted territory in the garden. This behavior is a directly derived from that of its wild relatives, in which establishing and defending territories is literally a matter of life and death.*

Above: *The cat's wonderful sense of balance and superb agility enable it to walk confidently along the thinnest bough without fear of falling. You may even see a cat perched, apparently asleep, on the top of an uncomfortably narrow fence or wall.*

Left: Rolling and rubbing are common among cats. They may be marking out their territory by rubbing the head and face to release scent from the sebaceous glands. Rolling also forms part of the mating sequence. The female in heat will roll provocatively on the ground and tread with her front paws, calling loudly as a signal for the tom to approach. However, there are also certain plants that will cause your cat to roll in ecstasy – whether encountered in the garden or dried and stuffed into a soft toy to be played with in the house. Catnip, or catmint, (Nepeta cataria) causes the most extreme reaction although no one really seems sure why: some cats get extremely excited when exposed to catnip – rolling, sniffing and meowing. Others seem hardly affected at all. Valerian (Valeriana officinalis) is another herb that has a similar effect.

Above: A superbly athletic cat captured in mid leap. Remarkably, cats can jump up to five times their own height vertically and are equally agile when attempting a sudden and maybe less rehearsed or calculated pounce. If done well – and not every jump is perfect, sometimes ending instead in an undignified scramble of paws – a cat can launch itself quickly and accurately onto its prey, front legs outstretched ready to land neatly and seize the unwitting mouse, shrew or screwed-up ball of paper. It is the cat's strong muscles in the hindquarters that give it such a powerful initial thrust. As a cat crouches to spring, the hip, knee and ankle joints bend, and are then rapidly extended by the contraction of their muscles, propelling the body strongly forwards. These joints are designed to act powerfully only in one direction: that is, along the length of the body.

Left: *Washing takes up a fair amount of time in a domestic cat's life, just as it does among wild cats. The tongue is long and muscular, and very rough to the touch. This enables the cat to use it as its own 'brush and comb' for serious grooming sessions. The flexibility of the backbone also allows a cat to to reach the back of its body.*

Right: *The ears are quick to react to any danger signals. This lovely Tabby-point Siamese cat has clearly heard something of interest and has erected its ears to catch every nuance of the sound. The ears may twitch even when a cat is asleep, showing that it is alert to any possible threat.*

***Left:** It can be fascinating to watch a cat go through the instinctive movements of hunting its prey – even if it is only a ball of wool. The cat lowers its body and begins to slink along, getting lower and lower until the belly touches the floor. Never taking its eye from its quarry, it judges the distance then springs, keeping the hindlegs on the ground as it pounces with its front paws. Often, the cat will play with its prey for some time, tossing it from one paw to another or allowing it to escape just a short distance, before finishing it off. This may appear cruel in a home setting, but the cat is just following the behavior patterns of its wild cousins.*

Left: *Tabby has always been one of the most commonly seen color markings in cats and although there are many color variations, ranging from brown and black to blue, cream and silver, the pattern is divided into only two main groups: the more commonly seen classic, or blotched, tabby and the rarer striped mackerel shown here. All tabbies owe their distinctive multicolored markings to their wild antecedents that, like the present-day big cats - such as leopards and tigers - relied on their spots and stripes for camouflage in the struggle to survive. This is particularly so for the mackerel, a pattern seen in both African and European wild cats.*

Right: *A cat's whiskers are highly sensitive and act like antennae, detecting the presence of objects or movement. The slightest disturbance stimulates the nerve endings. Most cats have around a dozen whiskers on each upper lip, a few on the cheek and tufts over the eyes.*

Below: *The clear, unwinking stare of a cat, with its slit pupils and reputation for being able to see in the dark, has earned it the reputation of being all seeing and hypnotic. The eyes have evolved for hunting and register all the available light in the dimmest of conditions.*

Life cycle of the cat

There is no mistaking a queen in heat. She howls and cries and is generally restless, which brings all the unneutered toms in the neighborhood to your door. If she is a pedigree cat and you wish to breed from her, this is the time to take her to the stud. If you intend to register the kittens, make all the necessary arrangements, such as choosing a suitable father, in advance. Mating follows a sequence of ritual movements and normally continues at intervals over several days. The male instinctively knows when to approach and when to withdraw. The kittens are born about nine weeks after conception and this usually presents few problems. The queen may prefer to give birth in a spot of her own choosing in the house and totally ignores the custom-made kittening box you have so thoughtfully provided. If she cannot be persuaded to use the box, lay down disposable bedding and make sure the area is warm, supplying an infrared lamp if necessary. A certain percentage of kittens are born tail first, and this is no cause for concern. The number of kittens per litter usually depends on the breed, and they may be born a few minutes or several hours apart. As soon as each kitten is born, the mother bites the cord and cleans them. They should suckle instinctively and during the first three weeks of their life the mother will feed, groom and encourage them to defecate. If you pick up the new kittens during this period, do not take them from the mother for long and teach every member of the household, especially young children, how to pick up and carry a kitten correctly. The new arrivals quickly become independent and you should provide them with warm bedding and a litter tray from the earliest opportunity. Later on, the kittens can be trained to use a cat flap. They will be ready to take a little solid food from about three weeks old. All kittens should be inoculated against the most dangerous infectious diseases from the age of about two months, and if you are not intending to breed from them, they can be neutered at five to six months. The kittens begin to play at about five weeks and their antics can be highly entertaining. Watch their first attempts to groom themselves, too. All kittens will be fully weaned by eight weeks. At this stage, the kitten will have all its milk teeth and will be experimenting with stalking, pouncing and scooping. As your kittens grow and develop, you will see them practicing and perfecting their instinctive skills. A pedigree cat will soon develop its breed characteristics, be it a capricious Siamese or a good-natured Burmese.

Left: *A Golden Longhair kitten. A young cat will not usually be totally independent until it is six months old.*

Right: *The mother normally keeps her kitten warm and well fed and cleans and grooms it for the first few weeks. Should the queen be unable or reluctant to cope, be prepared to undertake these tasks yourself.*

Right: *The tom ejaculates as soon as he has covered the queen and then he withdraws to wait and watch her at a discreet distance. The female continues to roll and rub herself for five to fifteen minutes, and then the mating sequence begins again. This may take place many times a day while the queen is in heat, and the stud cats may be left together for two to three days. If the queen does not conceive, she will be in estrus again in two to three weeks.*

Right: *When the queen is ready for mating, she raises her rump provocatively and pedals with her front feet on the ground. Only when he sees this stance will the tom dare to mount her, grasping the scruff of her neck between his teeth. Before this stage the female may be quite hostile, spitting and clawing at the male, who wisely keeps his distance. He calls to her at intervals until she relents and begins the rolling and purring sequence that is his signal she is ready to mate.*

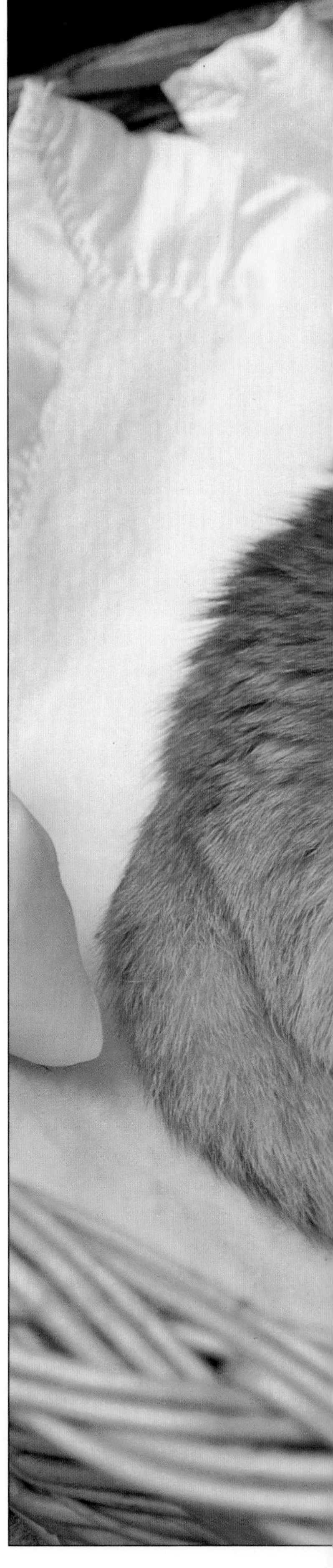

Right: *Once all the kittens are born and have been cleaned, they will want to suckle the mother. It is vital that they are allowed to do this as soon as possible, because the colostrum they receive in the first few days is rich in proteins and minerals. It also contains antibodies that help protect the young kittens from disease. When the litter is large, one kitten may get pushed out and not gain weight as rapidly as it should; if it seems healthy and normal in every other respect, you will have to hand rear it. Weaning can start after about three weeks when the kittens have grown some milk teeth and are beginning to stand on their own feet.*

Right: *Kittens can be sexed at about three weeks old, when they have grown their first milk teeth and are starting to look more like young cats. Sexing is done by holding the kitten away from you and lifting the tail for a closer examination. There are two openings in both the male and female, but they are much closer together in the female. The opening nearest the tail is the anus. In the female, you may be able to identify the vulva, which almost adjoins the anus, but it is not easy to distinguish in a young kitten. In the male, the penis is concealed in a small round opening separated from the anus by the scrotal sacs, which are not normally visible until the kitten is about six weeks old. Naturally it is much easier to sex an adult cat.*

Left: *It will not be long before a kitten begins to take on the breed characteristics of its parents. If both of them were carefully matched pedigree purebreds, the young cat should be true to type. This is important if you intend to breed cats for showing. These Russian Blues, for example, should ideally develop a slender but muscular body, with large ears and small, slightly rounded feet. The coat must be an even blue shade, with a wonderful silver sheen. There have been experiments with breeding a white variety, but it was not popular. A certain temperament tends to be inherited from the parents, as well as their looks, and the Russian Blue should prove to be a quiet, shy cat, happy to lead an indoor life and obedient enough to train on a collar and lead.*

Right: *When the kitten is about three weeks old, it will begin to take its first tentative steps, followed a week or so later by the ability to run and play. As soon as it can walk and is confident enough to explore further afield, a kitten will love to venture outdoors, especially if its mother comes too. This will not only introduce the young cat to new sights, smells and sounds, but also encourages it to develop many of its essential physical skills, such as stalking, climbing and scratching. Most mature cats are just as playful as they were as kittens. Very young kittens should only be allowed to go outside if the weather is really fine. If you intend to use a cat flap or similar pet door to allow free access to the garden, push the kitten gently through it a few times in both directions, until it gets the idea of how to use it.*

Left: *Kittens can be hand-reared if necessary, using a dropper syringe or specially shaped feeder bottle, which has a teat designed as closely as possible to resemble that of the nursing queen. These are available from pet shops and veterinary suppliers. Good hygiene is essential to avoid the risk of infection, so prepare each feed with fresh ingredients and sterilize all the utensils. You can buy a feline milk substitute or use proprietary milk powder or evaporated milk mixed as recommended by your veterinarian. You will need to feed the kittens every two hours for the first three weeks, although after the first few days, you can usually persuade them to accept four-hourly feeds during the night.*

Left: These Abyssinian kittens will grow into irresistibly handsome, lithe-bodied adults, with large almond shaped eyes and big pointed ears, completely different from any other kind of shorthaired cat. Play is very important to a cat's early development and if the mother or sibling kittens are not on hand to help with the education process, it is important that the kittens are handled for at least ten minutes a day and given plenty of toys or other objects to play with. Watching the antics of a six to eight week old kitten as it chases its own tail, pounces on imaginary rodents or indulges in a mock fight, can be highly amusing.

Right: This delightful Silver Tabby Longhair kitten will enjoy exploring its new surroundings. A small garden or backyard with a few green plants and some soil to scratch about in will provide the growing cat with all the fun and exercise it needs. Hunting small rodents through the undergrowth is as exciting as life in any jungle and there will be plenty of opportunities to protect the 'home patch' from intruders, such as other cats. If there are no trees in your garden, erect a wooden frame to provide the correct exercise, as well as protect your furniture from scratching.

Above: *Even where the parents are carefully matched as part of a deliberate breeding program, the litter will be a mixed bunch of colors and patterns - sometimes the coat length varies in the odd kitten too. By isolating an interesting color or type and selectively breeding, a new variety might be developed. These Angoras are coming back into fashion after almost becoming extinct.*

Below: *A Blue Longhair cat with her kitten. Every kitten is a darling and will win your heart as soon as you catch its cheeky eye. But do try to come home with a cat that is going to suit your inclinations and lifestyle. Not everyone finds they can live with a long-haired breed that takes a lot of grooming and leaves hairs all over the furniture. Some breeds just aren't suited to a mostly indoor life. Be sure to teach children how to handle any pet cats in the home.*

Right: *Tiny Maine Coon kittens prepare to face the world. Their eyes are fully open after 8-20 days, by which time they have started to crawl around their basket or box. All kittens are born with blue eyes, which do not begin to change until the cat is about 12 weeks old. Do not remove kittens from their mother until they are about 6-8 weeks old.*

All kinds of cats

Faced with choosing a cat for yourself or simply visiting one of the big international shows, the variety seems endless and deciding which you like the best is well-nigh impossible. There are big fluffy cats and small sleek ones, long-legged cats and short squat types with pugnacious faces. Their coats are marked with spots, stripes and patches and occur in every conceivable color, from black or white to red, blue, lilac, silver and gold. Cat breeders are introducing new colors all the time to extend the existing range, and some win instant acclaim, while others take decades to become accepted. Yet, unlike dogs, there are not that many different basic cat types, merely specially developed variations of a few standard body shapes and characteristics. Consider physique, for example. Under all that fur, the velvety Siamese or fluffy Persian, the wrinkly hairless Sphinx and curly Rex all fall into two main body shapes: either the cobby, flat-faced cats, with rounded heads and plump cheeks or the sleek, foreign type, with their unmistakably oriental, wedge-shaped heads, lithe slender bodies and long, slim legs with dainty paws. Some breeds are modifications of one of these types or a blend of both: the foreign-looking Burmese, for example, has a much rounder, fuller figure than the typically oriental breed. Because cats naturally keep themselves fit, they tend to maintain their correct body shape, only becoming obese if overfed and underexercised by doting owners. Tails and ears tend to follow body type; they are smaller and rounder on the cobby cat, but large and pointed on the oriental. Again, there are variations: the Scottish Fold, for example, has ears that are flattened against its head like a comical cap, and the Manx has no tail at all. Then there is fur type; strictly speaking, cats are either longhaired or shorthaired, depending on whether they originated in a warm country or a cold one, but long hair might be soft and silky or thick and coarse. Short fur can be as plush as a top quality carpet, or short and fine as in the coat of the Foreign Shorthair. Color is controlled by the cat's genes and as the breeders' understanding of genetics increases, the range of shades within the different breeds becomes more widespread. Cats that are, say, completely white, black, red or blue are called self-colored; cats that are white plus another color are described as bicolors. Certain cats have hairs tipped with a second color, which produces a lovely shimmering, smoky effect, and the trademark of the Siamese is the contrasting color on the 'points' - the nose, ears, feet, mask and tail. Tortoiseshell and tabby markings combine several colors in patches, stripes and spots, echoing the camouflage of the wild cat breeds. Today, colors and markings are largely controlled by deliberate breeding programs, but originally they were intended to blend in with the animal's background and to send important signals. The markings around a cat's face are intended to emphasize its expression; for example, dark lines around the mouth maximize a snarl. A queen (the term applied to a female cat) often has a dark tip to her tail, making it easy for the kittens to follow her safely through long grass.

Above: *The Siamese cat remains a popular choice with prospective owners. Not only do they appreciate its elegant good looks and contrasting color markings, but they also enjoy its strong character and the playful nature that makes it such an entertaining pet.*

Left: *A Silver Red Devon Rex. This breed is lively, entertaining and affectionate and has the added advantage that it requires little grooming. Simply comb the fur gently once a week and hand groom it as required by stroking the hair firmly from neck to tail.*

Right: *Many people find the Birman's exotic good looks irresistible, with its long silky coat and colored points as its most distinguished features. The Birman is more refined than most cobby longhaired breeds, but broader and more muscular than the true oriental type of cat.*

Left: The Burmese is descended from a Foreign type brown female imported to the US from Burma in the 1930s and mated with a Siamese in the absence of a suitable male. Shown here are a classic Brown Burmese and one of the new colors that have become increasingly popular, the Platinum, sometimes called a Lilac. Its beautiful pink-gray color is emphasised by its thick, short coat. This color, along with the Champagne, or Chocolate, was first bred in the United States in the late 1960s to 1970s and is difficult to distinguish until the cat is several weeks old.

Right: Non-pedigree cats come in all shapes and sizes and are usually chosen purely for their color and markings, unlike pedigree cats, whose temperament can be predicted.

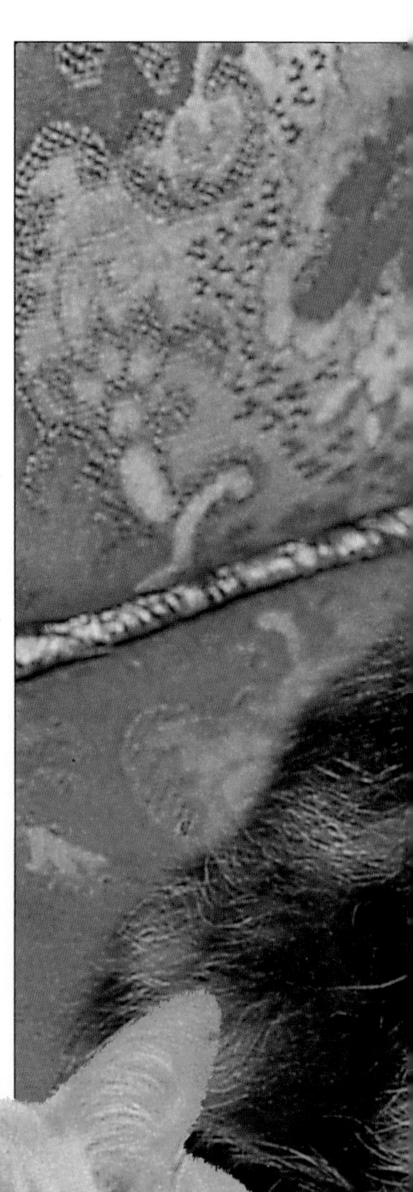

Below: The Burmese is valued mostly for its glossy, smooth, short coat. Although it is a foreign type, the Burmese has a well-rounded body, which combined with the coat, gives the cat a wonderfully plush appearance and brings out the coloring. Here, a rich Chocolate and a Cream enjoy each other's company. They have no other markings, but the Burmese is available in tortie variations, giving a more patchy appearance. In total there are nine variations, all of which have yellow eyes. Breeders in the USA prefer the cat to have a good rounded body, head and eyes.

Right: Bicolor Longhairs come in any recognized solid color combined with white, but perhaps one of the best loved combinations is the striking 'magpie' or black-and-white. In a pedigree cat, bicolors are preferred where between one third and one half of the fur is white, but variations in which the color is restricted to the extremities can be acceptable. Sometimes a cat may look black-and-white, but is in fact a tortoiseshell, with no or at least no visible red patches.

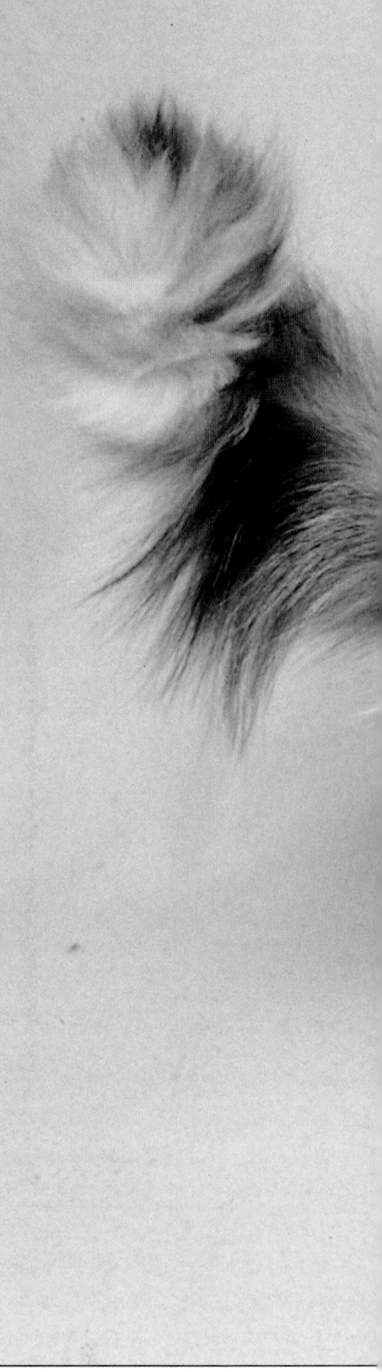

Left: *Some of the colors achieved in cats through selective breeding are quite extraordinary. Who would have thought it possible to produce the sparkle of this Chinchilla? These cats belong to the silver group of Longhairs and are named after the South American rodent whose dark undercoat is tipped with white. However, in the cats, the situation is reversed.*

Right: *A lovely soft blue color is seen to great effect in this Foreign type breed. Self blue cats do occur naturally in litters from time to time, and it is these that have been selected to breed today's blue tinged pedigrees. There are several recognized blues among the oriental body type cats, including the silvery Russian Blue and the Korat. Blue Shorthairs include the British Shorthair and the silvery French Chartreuse.*

Above: *Longhaired cats are undoubtedly beautiful, but they do involve a lot of extra care and grooming if they are to remain looking at their best. Most of today's pedigree Longhairs are descended from cats brought to the UK from Turkey and Persia in the late 19th century and are also called Persians. This Silver Tabby is one of many superb modern color variations.*

Left: *The domestic shorthaired tabby is everyone's idea of the homely fireside family pet. In fact, of all the cats, it bears the closest resemblance to its tiger-striped or mackerel tabby wild cat ancestor, which is the origin of all domestic cats, whether they be the classic, or blotched, type of tabby or any of the other cat colors where the tabbiness is suppressed. Red and brown tabbies are the most familiar, but the tabby variation can be found in any of the main self colors.*

Left: *One of the most stunning Longhaired varieties is the Black-tipped Smoke, with its large, pale ruff set against a dense coat of silky, jet black tipped fur. It has often been a championship winner. Like all Smokes, the tips are so long that at first the cat appears to be a solid color. Only when it moves does the paler undercoat become visible, producing a stunning shimmering effect. There is also a Blue-tipped Smoke variety.*

Below: *The Siamese's eastern origins are strikingly evident in its regal, wedge-shaped head, elegant legs and lithe body, tapering into a long tail. The elegant legs are long and slim with dainty paws. Its short, fine fur shows off its pretty colors, as in this Blue-point.*

Below: *Some cats do not conform exactly to one of the two main body types: lithe oriental (foreign) or stocky cob type. The Abyssinian, for example, is strictly speaking the foreign type, but it is not quite as lithe and elegant as that classic oriental cat, the Siamese. That is not to say it is not as good-looking or exotic - indeed, the Abyssinian is one of the most attractive breeds, with its slender but muscular long-tailed body and large pointed ears. The head is more of a rounded wedge shape - again a blend of types - with wonderfully expressive, almond-shaped eyes. The short, extremely thick coat is generally pale brown or black, but there is a also a Red and a Blue variety. Its distinctive good looks identify it as being related to the Sacred Cat once worshipped by the Ancient Egyptians. It has also earned a number of descriptive nicknames in the past, such as Rabbit cat or Bunny cat. Despite its impressive pedigree, it will enjoy a taste of the outdoor life.*

Below: *The Somali is a long-haired version of the exotic Abyssinian, and although its pedigree is not as long and distinguished, it is equally attractive, showing all the same basic physical characteristics and entertaining personality. Both the Somali and the Abyssinian are bright and lively and quick to learn a trick or two, and both make excellent companions. They are not suited to the confines of a small apartment with no garden. Despite the wonderful effect of the Somali's classic ticked coloring in a long, silky coat, it took some time to be recognized as a breed. Although developed as long ago as the 1930s, it was not officially accepted until the 1970s. The Somali's luxuriant coat gives it an almost wild appearance, but its character is completely civilized if vigorous. The 'Usual' Somali pictured here in the center, is a ruddy brown, ticked with darker brown or black, but there are other color variations including a Sorrel, or Red, as well as the Silver-blue of its two companions pictured here.*

Choosing a cat

Keeping a cat can bring enormous pleasure to young and old alike. However, if you have never owned a cat before, there are a few points to consider before you commit yourself. The most important thing to take into account is your own lifestyle and how that will fit in with being a cat owner. For instance, although a cat does not need the same degree of attention as a dog, you will still have to find the time to take care of it and feed it properly. Some types of cat need more care than others. If you travel a great deal for business or pleasure and find little time to keep up with your domestic chores, you are unlikely to make a good cat companion. In a busy family, a cat's needs may be overlooked and the children may quickly lose interest in the daily responsibility of caring for it. On the other hand, many children are true animal lovers and the cat becomes their treasured pet. Perhaps you are elderly or housebound, with plenty of time on your hands. If they are accustomed to your company from a kitten, some cats make excellent house companions in return for a little love and care. The next thing to decide is what kind of cat to keep. If you have set your heart on a particular pedigree breed, perhaps because you like its looks or character or because you want to show or breed from it, be prepared to pay quite a price. Alternatively, if you simply want an attractive household friend, your local pet shop or even cat sanctuary is sure to be able to meet your requirements for a fraction of the cost. Sometimes you see cards advertised on the pinboard at your veterinary clinic. However, you should not bring home the first furry bundle that tugs at your heartstrings. Remember that longhaired cats take more time to look after than shorthaired ones. Daily grooming may be necessary to keep that coat in good condition. Longhaired cats also leave a lot of hair around the house, adding to your daily household chores. Some cats are more suited to an apartment life, while others need constant access to the outdoors. Before you bring your chosen cat home, make sure you have catered for its particular needs by removing any potential hazards and equipping it with a litter tray (or box), cat flap, toys and scratching post. Your cat will also need somewhere warm and comfortable to sleep, as well as feeding bowls and a supply of suitable food. If the cat is still very young, be prepared to spend some time with it in the first few months, amusing it, training it and helping it to settle in. If you have more than one kitten, preferably from the same litter, they will settle in more quickly and generally be more contented. It is important to have your cat examined and inoculated by a veterinarian, and if you do not intend to breed from it, have it neutered or spayed. Unneutered males can be a particular nuisance, spraying urinary signals around the garden and on the furniture, getting into fights over females and being generally more aggressive.

Right: *Despite its inbred independent nature, the cat that has grown up with a young family and is used to being handled can make a loving companion, enjoying a cuddle at any time and even joining in the children's games with relish.*

Below left: *For the right person, a Longhair, such as this Brown Classic Tabby, makes a splendid and handsome companion, maybe capable of winning rosettes if it is a pedigree and you are interested in showing cats. Always remember that a show cat needs lots of attention and perfect credentials to be in with a chance of success.*

Right: *A kitten in the family can be great fun, especially once it has begun to explore the big world outside its box or basket. You should spend some time every day playing with your new cat, as this will teach it important skills and provide it with the exercise to keep fit and healthy. This is particularly important if yours is a single cat: if you are lucky enough to have a couple of kittens the same age, they will happily keep each other occupied, playing, pouncing and having mock fights - antics that will amuse you too. It may be worth considering how many cats you are prepared to have at the outset: buying from the same litter is always preferable to introducing a new kitten into a household with an older cat already well established.*

Left: *If you have plenty of time to spare for your pet, you may be interested in buying a longhaired cat. Kept in good condition, the long, silky coat is a real eye-catcher, and these cats are available in wonderful colors and patterns, such as this handsome tabby. It takes regular grooming to keep this fine fellow looking so good, but it is well worth the trouble if you like to surround yourself with beautiful things. Daily brushing also helps to prevent the coat molting around the home. Always remember to support your cat properly in your arms when carrying it around and never tease or aggravate it. This is a lesson for everyone in the house to learn.*

Right: *Siamese kittens are quick developers, opening their eyes at only a few days old and venturing away from the mother within three to four weeks of being born. They are demanding and sometimes capricious companions, but given plenty of attention, they make amusing and playful pets. The point coloring - that is, the color on the nose, ears, feet and tail that usually contrasts strongly with the plain body color - takes some time to develop, and even their true eye color will not be known for about eight weeks, as all Siamese kittens are born with blue eyes. They are as intelligent as their alert expression suggests and can even be taught to do tricks.*

Left: *Of course, if you are not fussy about what breed of cat you own there are a great many fine non-pedigree types to choose from, at a fraction of the cost of a pure breed. 'Truffles' here is certainly a handsome example of a happy and well cared for cat.*

Right: *Be prepared for your cats to take over the place! A cat in the house means any convenient perch or receptacle is fair game for a nap. Knowing her cat's preferences, this considerate owner has made sure that the bread is stored elsewhere and that there is a tasty snack of home-grown herbs and grasses to prevent her houseplants being nibbled.*

Left: *Despite their reputation for being rather offhand, if you have cared for your cat since it was young, it will grow to be a loving and loyal friend. Indeed, many can become very affectionate companions for those who cannot get out much. Although a cat does not require as much attention as a dog, its needs must be carefully considered, especially if it will be housebound. It is best to introduce a kitten to this kind of lifestyle and not a fully grown cat that may have been used to a more outdoor life. You will need a place for food, water and a litter tray, which will require attention every day, and some kind of scratching post to prevent your cat attacking the furniture.*

Right: *Be prepared to spend plenty of time with brush and comb if you choose a longhaired breed. In the wild, such cats would only molt in winter, but in the artificially heated environment of your home they will lose their hair all year round. They will need two daily sessions or the coat will become a mass of tangles and the cat will have to be professionally shaved by a veterinarian to get rid of them. You will need a special pet's grooming brush and a couple of combs; show cats have specialized brushes to bring them up to peak condition.*

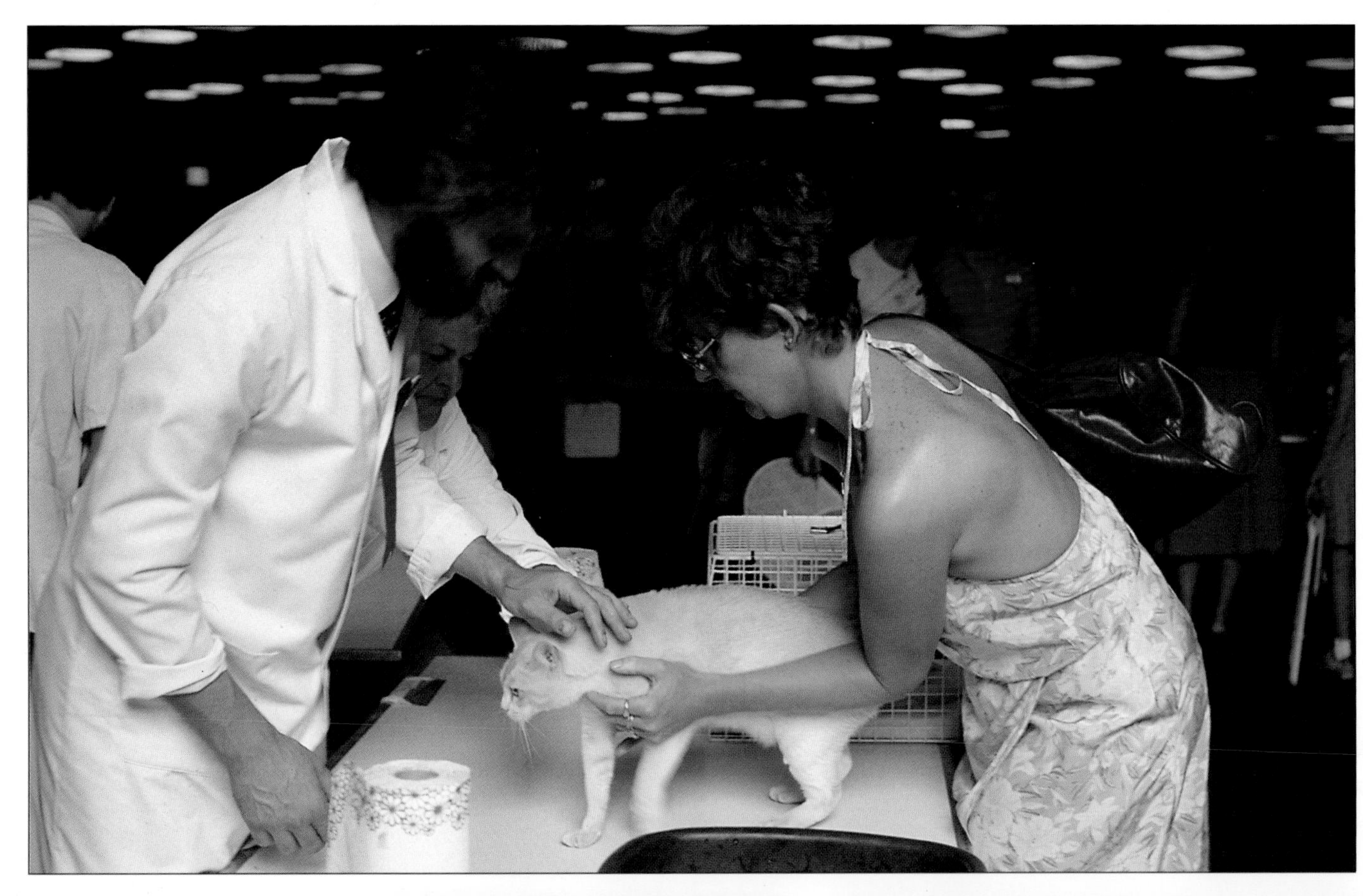

***Left:** On show day, the judges will assess each cat on two main areas: how closely it conforms to breed type and its general appearance and condition. Standards are set for each breed and points are awarded, usually totalling a maximum of 100. The highest scoring cat is declared the champion. If there is a tie, the cats will be judged again directly against each other, concentrating mainly on their general appearance. Standards are extremely high, with the intention of selecting an absolutely perfect specimen, so faults that may seem comparatively minor to the owner could be enough to disqualify the animal right from the start. You should be familiar with your breed's requirements before entering.*

***Right:** Cat shows date back over a hundred years and became popular after the big show at Crystal Palace in London in 1871. The first shows in North America began around the same time in New England and took off after a show in Madison Square Gardens in 1895. The system was very similar to one used now, the cats being judged in individual pens with cards awarded to the winners. However, without modern vaccinations and veterinary medicine, showing could be a risky business, putting your cat at risk of catching some fatal disease. Today, you will not be allowed to show your cat unless you can produce the necessary vaccination documents. Shown here is one of the biggest championship shows in the world: the National Cat Club Show held in London every December.*

Right: ***Right:*** *Show points are awarded for different physical characteristics depending on breed. The judge will probably look first at the head, assessing the shape and angle of the ears, the nose and jaw, comparing them with the standards set. Shape of the face, fullness of the cheeks and tilt of the muzzle are all considered. The eyes are judged separately for size, shape and color, but also for their health and brilliance, whether they are set far apart and the expression they give to a cat's face. The body must be true to type: either stocky and cobby but not coarse; or elegantly oriental, slender while still muscular, without seeming too thin. Legs, paws and tail must be in proportion and carried according to the standard.*

Caring for your cat

Despite its reputation for being fiercely independent, there is more to caring for a cat than feeding it occasionally, turning it out of the house at night and leaving it to fend for itself while you go on vacation. After all, a cat is a domesticated animal and it is your responsibility to ensure that it has a balanced diet and is able to exercise. Of course, some cats are better at looking after themselves than others; often, these skills are inherited or learnt from the mother. However, many pedigree cats require a great deal of attention from their owners if they are to remain in peak condition. While most domesticated cats will exercise their ancient instincts by hunting small birds, mice and other rodents, only a few hardy farm cats have the skill and experience to sustain themselves totally on what they can kill. You will find that your enterprising pet will be more likely to scrounge off your neighbors than try and 'live off the land'. Whether you own a show cat or an undistinguished family pet, the two most important requirements to consider are food and drink. There are a great many different types of food on the market for cats, from canned and dried meals to semi-moist mixtures, and you may have to experiment with a selection until you find one or more products that your cat likes and which are convenient for you to serve. Try to vary the diet as much as possible, as a cat may become addicted to one type or even one variety of food, which is both inconvenient for you and bad for the animal. Many brands offer a wide choice, from liver, rabbit and beef to several kinds of fish. Try changing brands occasionally, as well as flavors. Fresh water should be available at all times, but consider milk as a food rather than a drink, and remember that some cats are allergic to cow's milk. Opinion is divided when it comes to letting a cat out at night or not. Unneutered toms will fight mercilessly to defend their territory or win the favors of a queen in heat, returning home, sometimes after several worrying days, lighter in weight and with parts of their anatomy in shreds. If your cat is a pedigree or has particularly fine coat markings, you run the risk of it being stolen by cat thieves, who think nothing of converting your pet into a piece of marketable fur. In busy towns and cities, of course, there is also the risk of a traffic accident. A feed at dusk is often sufficient to lure your cat indoors. Any cat confined within the home for any length of time should be provided with a litter box, and this must be renewed regularly as cats are fastidious creatures. If you do not want it napping in your own bed or favorite armchair, provide a comfortable box or basket with a blanket or other bedding material for the cat to sleep in. When you take a vacation, you may have to consider boarding your pets if family and friends are not prepared to help out.

Above: *The farm cat is largely self-reliant and needs very little attention, being tough, hardy and independent. It will work hard for its living too, eagerly keeping down the local rodent and rabbit population, so take care not to poison these pests.*

Left: *You can tell immediately when a cat is well cared for: it looks sleek and shiny, and it will display that typical cat contentment, happy simply to while away the day as if in a dream.*

Right: *Most cats enjoy fresh air and will play for hours in your garden hunting imaginary prey but hopefully not digging up too many of your prize plants.*

Left: *Scratching the furniture is one of the most annoying habits the indoor cat can develop and should be stopped at the earliest possible age. Do not look on it indulgently as the antics of a playful kitten - later on your grown cat will reduce your soft furnishings to shreds and destroy any polished wooden furniture. A young cat with unrestricted access to a garden should soon learn not to be a nuisance if given a sharp reprimand. If your pet is mostly housebound, you will have to provide a scratching post and teach it to use this rather than the furniture. Some US cat owners have their cat's claws surgically removed - it is illegal in other countries - but this seems an unnecessarily harsh measure.*

Right: *A scratching post is essential for the apartment cat. You can buy one from any good pet shop or make your own. Some are quite elaborate, involving a largish wooden framework, big enough for the cat to climb on and exercise its muscles, as well as its claws. However, if all you want is a simple post, this need only be 12-24in(30-60cm) high and covered in rough bark or a similar synthetic rough surface. Some posts are covered in cork impregnated with catnip to encourage the cat to use it. You can cover the post in carpet, but this will need replacing regularly. Mount the post on a heavy base to stop it tipping over, as cats prefer a vertical surface. If you are very short of space, screw a piece of bark or carpet to the wall.*

Left: *Your cat will find plenty to occupy itself outside, even in a tiny backyard. Any tangle of plants is good for stalking and prowling, while a tree is marvelous for scratching or chasing birds. Cats love to climb, but are not quite as proficient at getting down again. Be prepared to carry out a rescue if yours appears to be stuck or in distress.*

Below: *Your cat may pick up all kinds of infestation in the garden, not just cat fleas, but also dog fleas, rabbit mites and even bird fleas. In a warm, dry, centrally heated home these multiply at an alarming rate. Be suspicious if you see your cat having a good scratch. If it does have an infestation, you will have to treat the animal, burn its bedding and clean its favorite lounging spots by vacuuming every day and washing walls and floors with disinfectant and washing soda to kill the eggs. Cats may also pick up an internal parasite, such as worms, from contaminated soil, mice, rats or beetles. Always pay strict attention to hygiene and have your cat regularly dewormed by a veterinarian.*

Below: There are various external cat parasites that will not only irritate your pet – and scratching will often be the first sign you have of the presence of these microscopic organisms – but may also cause further problems in the shape of disease and infection should they puncture the skin. It is important to identify such parasites as early as possible. During regular grooming, look out for fleas, ticks and mites and if you suspect a problem, begin treatment straight away. If in any doubt, contact your veterinarian for advice on the appropriate pesticide spray, powder or shampoo to use.

Below: Grooming a short-haired cat is quite quick and easy. A regular and thorough combing of the fur underneath is useful for removing any tangled twigs or burrs the cat has picked up outside. These may eventually begin to irritate the cat and cause problems.

Left: *Although your cat is perfectly capable of cleaning itself with its specially adapted tongue, you may need to give it a special shampoo to prevent infestation with parasites or to remove substances, such as sticky grease or oil, that may have become stuck to the coat and may be toxic if licked. If the cat has been used to being washed by you from an early age, this should not pose any problems. However, if the experience is a new one, it is usually a good idea to get someone to help you, as most cats hate getting wet and will struggle to get free. A hand spray is useful for rinsing.*

Below: *If your cat cannot tolerate getting wet, try giving it a 'dry shampoo' or bran bath. This is only practical for shorthaired cats with fur that is not too dirty. The bran is available from animal feed and pet suppliers. Heat 1-2lb (0.5-1kg) of bran in an oven at 300°F(150°C) for 20 minutes. Stand your cat on a newspaper and massage the warm bran into its coat against the growth and making sure the back, belly and tail are well covered. When completely covered, leave for as long as the cat will tolerate it, then simply comb out and groom the coat as normal.*

Left: *Most cats benefit from being allowed access to a garden or backyard, if only for limited periods every day. The fresh air and exercise are important to general health, as well as offering the chance to develop instinctive skills.*

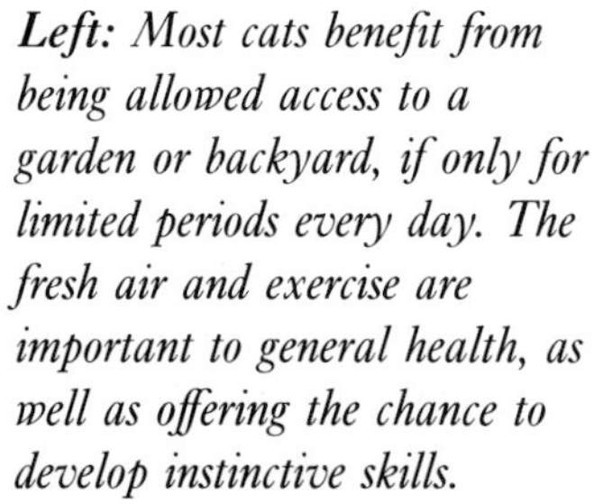

Left: *All cats are designed to feed off freshly killed prey, and domestic cats need a well-balanced diet that includes protein, vitamins and minerals. It is even more important for a costly pedigree to receive the right nutrients if it is to stay healthy and in good condition. The protein content of the diet is particularly important, as cats need twice as much as dogs. A cat's system is not very well equipped to cope with toxins, and this includes certain food preservatives. Too much of one food such as liver may also cause an imbalance or even poisoning. Plenty of variety is safest – even if you feed your cat proprietary cat food, so do ring the changes.*

Below: *In the wild, a cat receives as much as 70 percent of its required water intake from eating its prey. Cats normally require about 1 fluid ounce of water per pound of their body weight per day (about 60ml per kilogram). If you feed your cat canned food, it will be receiving the greater part of this automatically. Semi-moist foods contain half as much water as canned foods, but keep better in the bowl; dry foods are only about 10 percent water and you must supply at least 7 fluid ounces (200ml) of fluid with every meal. However, fresh water should always be available. A cat does have the facility to concentrate its urine and thus save water if it is left without, but more usually it will find some way of satisfying its thirst. A cat allowed free access to outdoors should have no problem finding a puddle or even an ornamental pool, as here (look out fish!). But even indoors you may be surprised at your pet's ingenuity in getting its head under a dripping tap or dipping its paw into receptacles of water. If your cat is unwell for any reason and off its food, make sure it drinks plenty of fluids, even if you have to force it, to avoid dehydration.*

Above: *Bad habits can be trained out of your cat from an early age. Housebound cats may vandalize houseplants by digging them up or nibbling them. This is best avoided by providing a small pot or box of some tasty favorites of their own, such as catnip, chickweed or lawn grass, as shown here. Some popular houseplants are also poisonous to cats if eaten. They include* Dieffenbachia, Solanum capiscastrum *and* Hedera *(ivy) and should be avoided where there are cats.*

Below: *Where a cat flap is not practical or your cat is restricted to being indoors, you must provide a litter tray from the earliest age and train your cat how to use it - this does not take long, providing you do not keep switching the position of the tray. Be sure to change the litter regularly to keep it clean and fresh or the cat will not want to use it.*

Left: *A cat flap allows your pet to go in and out at will. Fit the flap so the cat can step through comfortably - it should not have to jump. There are various types on the market, all of which are quite easy to install. Most cat flaps open in both directions and are fitted with a spring or magnet so they shut automatically and does not cause a draft. If you are worried about other cats coming in, you can buy a cat flap that is triggered by a device on the cat's collar.*

Below: *For unwanted or lost cats not destined to roam the backstreets and sewers there is always the cat sanctuary. Here, with too many cats and not enough homes willing to take care of them, they are forever overcrowded and their keepers are only too willing for you to take your pick of a new pet -or two. Choosing one can be difficult - they all look so appealing - but after you have taken your sorry bundle of fur home, remember that it should be thoroughly checked as soon as possible by a veterinarian. Some sanctuaries make it a condition that you sign an undertaking that you will have the cat vaccinated and neutered - at your own expense - before you are allowed to take it away.*

The healthy cat

Like any other animal, cats are susceptible to catching certain diseases or becoming low and out of condition if not properly cared for. Responsible owners can keep such risks to a minimum by keeping their pets generally healthy through regular veterinary check-ups and looking out for signs of specific problems. It is a good idea to keep a record of your cat's health, and its treatments and inoculations. Considering the cat's naturally active lifestyle, it is only fair to say that as far as accidents and injuries are concerned, they generally have to take their chances. However, you can minimize these risks by adapting your home, maybe keeping the animal indoors if you live in an area with dense traffic and by ensuring that any accidents are treated promptly and professionally. Only a qualified veterinarian can judge the correct course of action, but a rudimentary knowledge of pet first aid may be useful until your cat can receive specialized attention. The most important precaution you can take, especially if your pet is allowed to roam freely and mix with other cats, is to have it regularly inoculated; the cost is minimal compared to the bill for treating a sick animal. As charges for veterinary services escalate, some owners are now insuring their cats against injury or sickness, so that they can give their pet the best possible treatment without having to worry about the cost. Despite being proficient at grooming themselves, all cats require occasional brushing and maybe a wash; the longhaired breeds may even need daily grooming. This is a good time to check on your cat's general health and condition; you can look for the evidence of ticks or fleas, any cuts or sores or unwelcome growths. A healthy cat is bright-eyed and contented. If your pet seems off-color and listless, is not eating or is drinking more than usual, these are signals that something is wrong. If symptoms such as sneezing, vomiting or diarrhea do not clear up within a day or so, you should contact your veterinarian immediately. The cat's coat should be glossy and clean - sometimes a cat will rip its tongue or get a foreign object stuck in its mouth and cannot groom itself properly. The nose should be dry and clean, the eyes free from mucus. The biggest danger to the housebound animal is boredom. In an attempt to amuse itself, a cat may play with any convenient 'toy', perhaps chewing an electric cord or eating a poisonous houseplant or a packet of tablets. Always bear in mind that cats are not well equipped to expel toxins.

Right: *Allowing your cat at least some time outdoors enables it to exercise many of its natural instincts, perhaps preventing listlessness and boredom. The cat is by nature a territorial animal; confined indoors with no other cats for company it will feel threatened should one intrude and will appear aggressive.*

Below: *Cats are prone to respiratory problems such as viral infections of the nose and throat - sometimes called 'feline flu'. If there is any sign of sneezing or coughing, or if your cat has a runny nose, you should have it examined immediately by a veterinarian because early treatment is your pet's only chance of survival.*

Below: *Professional advice and treatment are sometimes the only way that a sick cat may stand a chance of recovery. The eyes are susceptible to several different kinds of ailment, most of which can become so bad if left untreated that the cat can go blind in one or both eyes. Like most animals, the eyes of the cat secrete a small amount of mucus, which they usually disperse themselves by moistening their front paws with their tongue and washing it off quite effectively, as nature intended. However, if the eyes are continually watering or a crust forms, there is no question that there is something wrong with them and that prompt treatment is required. Do not wait for the eyes to get better on their own. Conjunctivitis, for example, is common in cats and should be treated promptly with the recommended saline eye-washes and antibiotic drops before the infections spreads.*

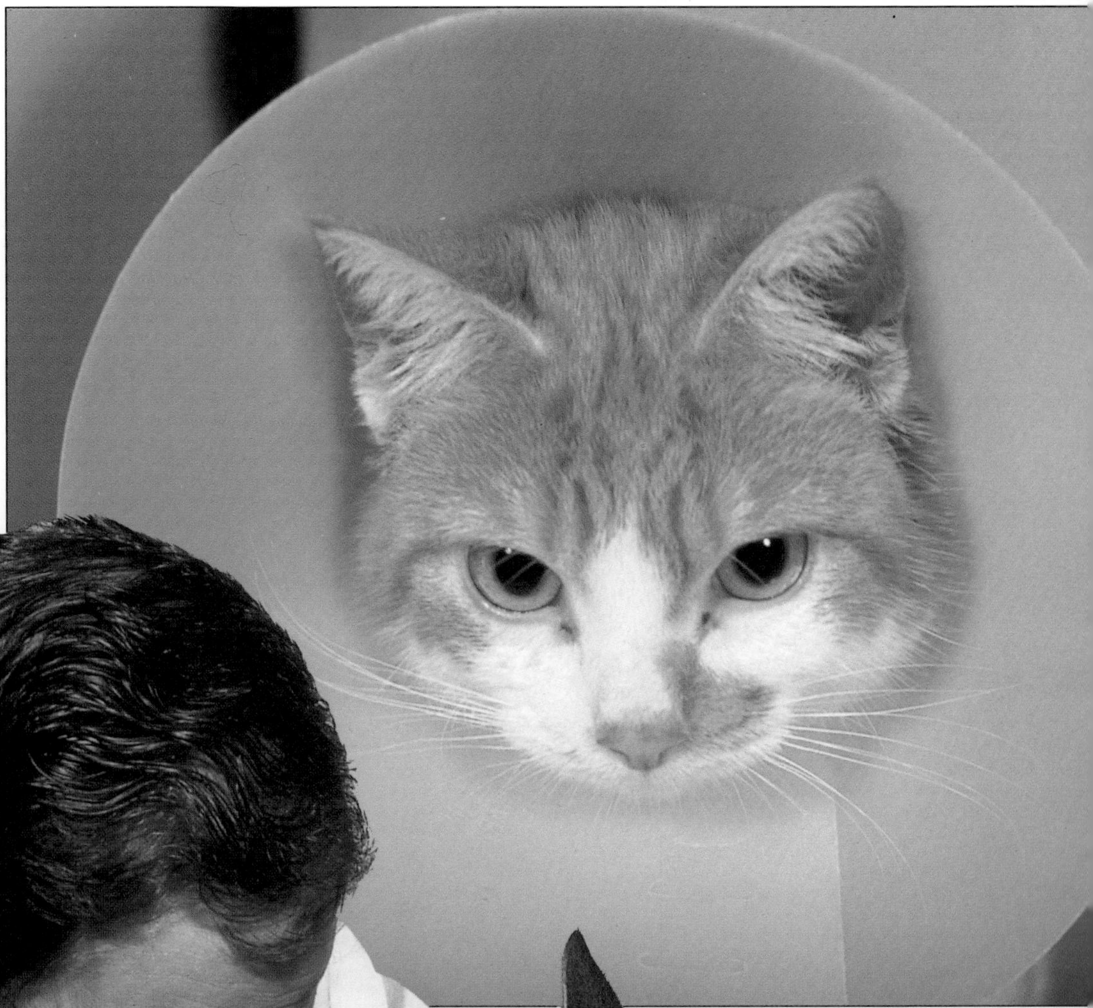

Left: *Skin problems can be a result of bacterial infection, an irritation caused by a chemical - perhaps in an impregnated flea collar - or a food allergy. After applying a medication, the cat may scratch or lick the treated area, preventing it from healing quickly. An Elizabethan collar fitted around the cat's neck will prevent the cat from reaching the area and doing any further harm. Such a collar is easy to make from a sheet of cardboard cut into part of a circle, leaving enough room for the cat's neck to move freely. Placed around its head, it can be taped to form the collar.*

Right: *As with any predatory animal, cats depend a great deal on hearing to assist them when hunting and in so many other aspects of everyday life. The ears are extremely sensitive organs that once damaged are seldom repairable. If you suspect your cat of having something wrong with its ears - you may have noticed it scratching them vigorously - do have them checked by your veterinarian as soon as possible.*

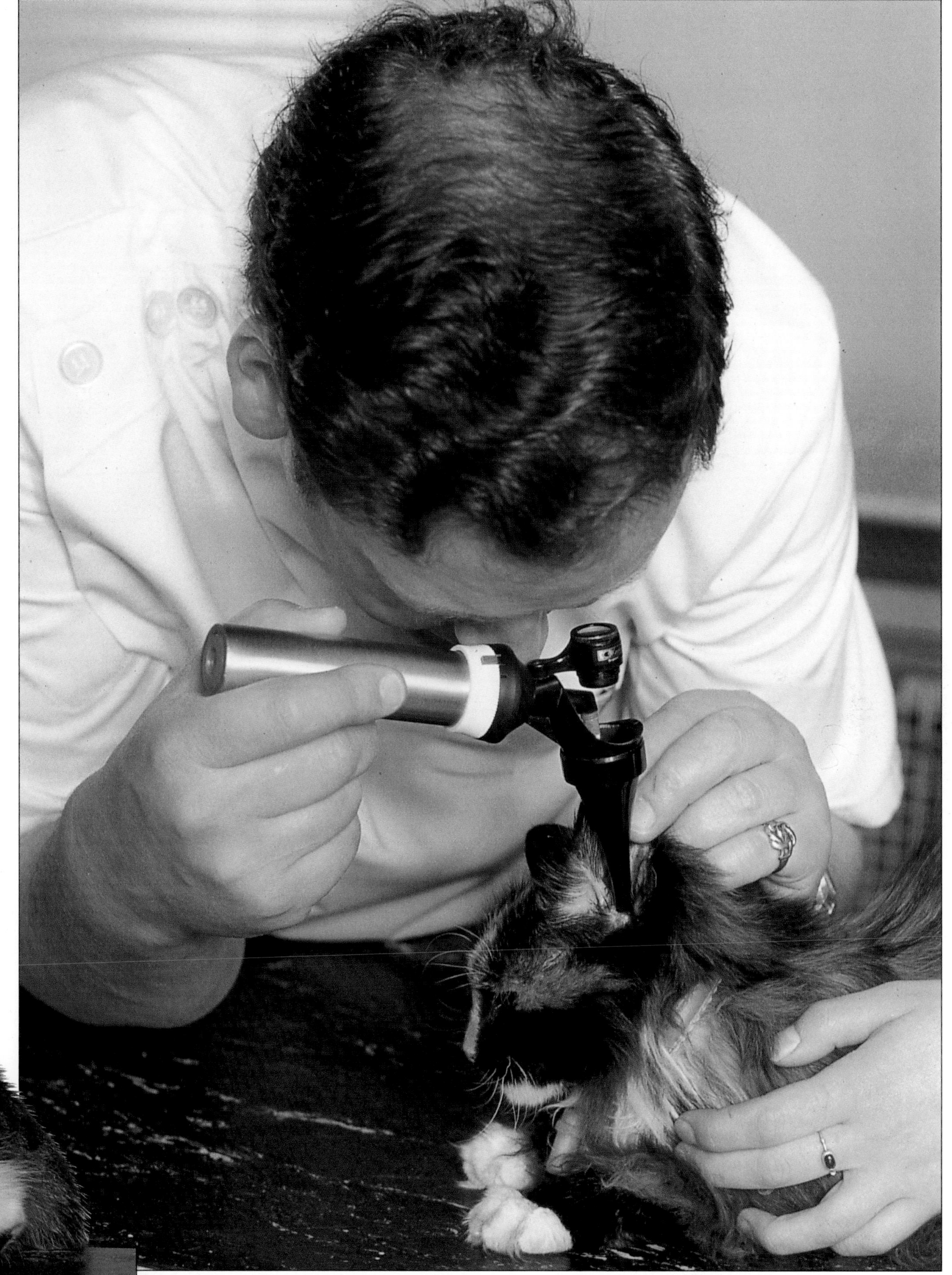

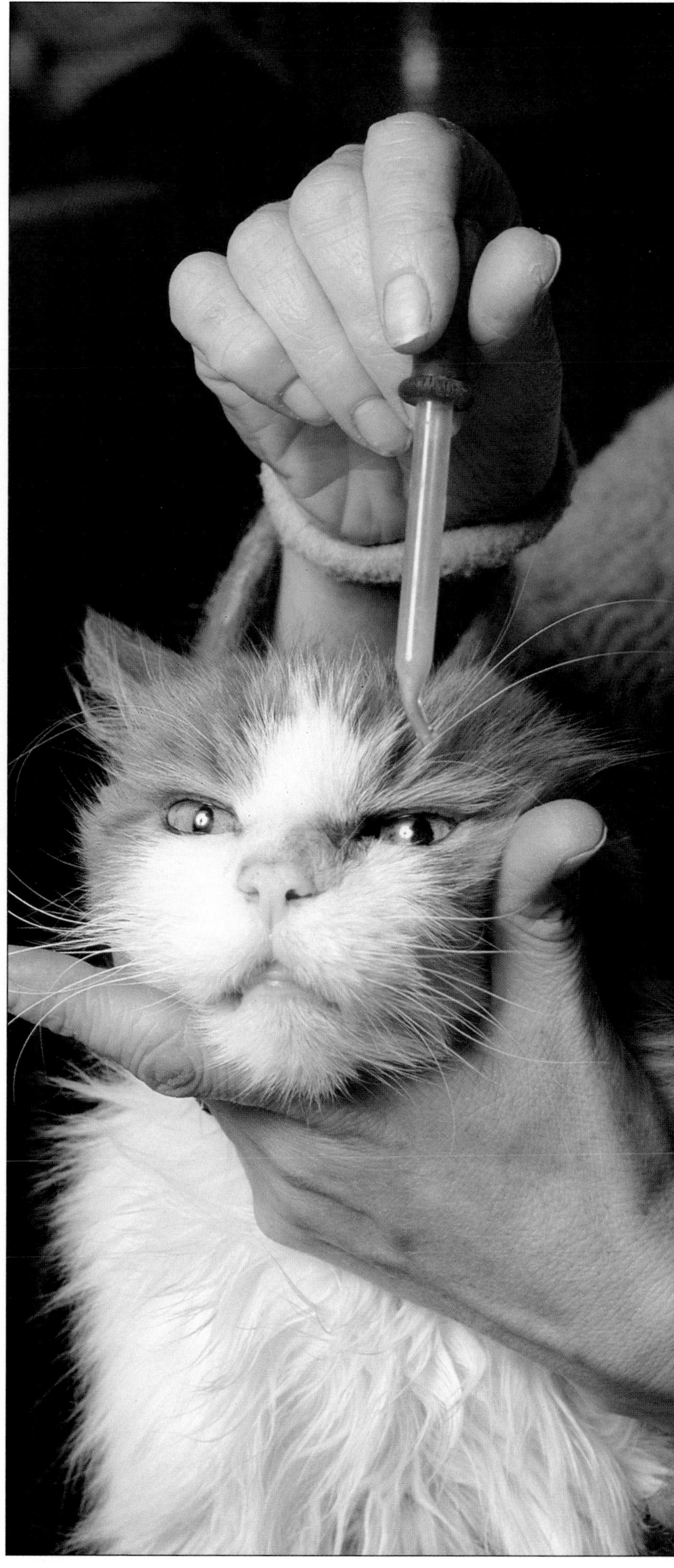

***Left:** Most cat owners are pretty well equipped when it comes to taking their cat to the veterinarian or on journeys where they feel it necessary to take their pet with them. The range of suitable baskets varies enormously, as does the price. Most of them are designed to fit into the rear or back seat of a car for easy transportation. Some cats enjoy riding in a car quite freely, but do not carry them unrestrained. The animals are also easier to control in a cage should your vehicle break down.*

***Above:** The eyes are extremely important to a cat's general well-being and ultimate survival. Without clear vision, a cat would not be able to hunt effectively or to defend itself, making it wretched even in a domestic situation. It is therefore essential to make sure that the eyes are cleaned and checked frequently for any possible ailments. Part of the regular grooming process should involve cleaning the eyes with a moist piece of absorbent cotton, as shown here.*

***Right:** You should only administer any kind of drugs or medical preparation to your pet if you have consulted a veterinarian first, perhaps to check your cat's eyes for a possible disorder, and he has recommended treatment. If he has prescribed eyedrops, apply these carefully as shown here while holding the cat firmly - get someone else to help you if necessary. After putting the eyedrops in, close the eyelids and gently massage the eyes to disperse the drops evenly around the eyeball.*

Above: Cats will benefit from a daily dose of fresh air and outdoor exercise. Sometimes it is possible to allow the animal free access via a cat flap or open window. Owners with a limited garden or backyard prefer to restrict their pet to a wire-mesh pen. This should be sheltered and part grass, part concrete with shelves and a scratching post if no tree is handy. Where this is not possible, you can exercise your cat on a lead, although only a few breeds will tolerate this.

Below: Some cat collars are purely ornamental - a velvet or even jewel-studded band to complement a pampered pet's coat color, sometimes with a lead to match. Many pedigree owners intending to show do not like to put a collar on their cat as it may mark the neck and lose them show points. Generally speaking, though, the collar is for identification purposes and if your cat is allowed to roam the neighborhood freely it is a good way to keep track of it should it stray. Some cats go off for weeks at a time, adopting another family for a few days. In these cases, a collar shows whether the cat is a stray or not. Identification is also useful in the sad event of an accident- and may even save your pet's life. Usually a tag or tube with the owner's address or telephone number on it is attached to the collar. Some soft-hearted owners even attach a bell to warn birds of the cat's approach. The collar must fit properly, not so loose that it can get caught, nor so tight that it rubs and chafes. Some collars are impregnated with chemicals to deter fleas, but these are not always a good idea as they can irritate the skin and their efficiency is limited in any case.

Above: *Mock fighting may look fierce but is in fact a valuable way for cats to practice essential aggressive and defensive techniques and to exercise their muscles. Such games may start between kittens as young as three to six weeks, when they will jump on one another, wrestle, kick, chase and pounce with great accuracy. If you watch carefully, you will see each take turns to be the aggressor.*

Right: *Although cats have more fun and are less likely to be bored if there is more than one of them, the single cat will still find plenty of ways to amuse and occupy itself. Kittens are notoriously mischievous, but even a mature cat retains its sense of playfulness and fun. It is a good idea to provide some kind of toys to play with to discourage cats making off with something you'd rather wasn't mauled. The lone cat will also chase its own tail, stalk imaginary foes and pounce on all manner of insects that come within reach.*

Below: *A young kitten may look lost and vulnerable in the wide open spaces of even the smallest backyard, but it is well equipped to look after itself and will soon learn how to stalk, hide and hunt. However, if you live in the country, it may be a different story, as there are many animals and birds that could prey on a small kitten before it is old enough to defend itself.*

Right: *You may notice your cat slowing down as it ages – every year of its life is said to equal seven of ours and so by the time it is eight years old it is well into middle age. This veteran cat of 21 years is still going strong, but some cats become fat and lazy, while others become scrawny. Old cats may become a little deaf or blind, and possibly incontinent. Keep them warm and give them plenty to drink, as the kidneys are prone to failure, but keep an eye open for excessive thirst, as this may be a sign of disease or diabetes. If your older cat becomes fussy about what it will eat, try giving it smaller, more frequent meals. If a cat becomes very frail or infirm, there may be little your veterinarian can do other than to recommend it is put down.*

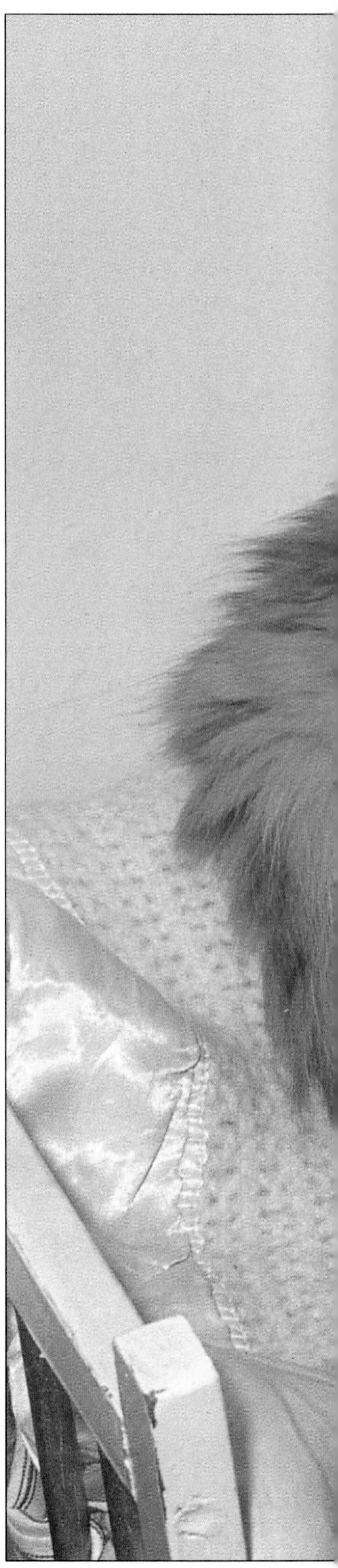

Shorthaired cats

One of the advantages of keeping a shorthaired cat is that its coat does not become matted or tangled and even a pedigree cat only needs a quick brush a couple of times a week to keep it looking smart. From the chunky Shorthair, with its plush coat and affectionate nature, to the exotic-looking and rare Korat, famous for its delicate heart-shaped face and big green eyes, there is plenty of choice of types, and especially colors and patterns, which are always displayed more dramatically on a short coat. The American Shorthair is a large, lean, hardy cat that is believed to have traveled to the Americas with the Pilgrim Fathers and subsequently interbred with local cats. This tough and athletic cat is available in a wide range of varieties, including bicolors, shaded coats, cameos, tabbies and tortoiseshells. The British Shorthair has a more rounded head, is slightly smaller but still muscular, and is just as good-natured and intelligent. If you are attracted by the beautiful shading or pattern detail of a shorthaired cat, plus its ease of grooming, but would prefer a pet that has a more exotic, less stocky appearance, then take a look at the Foreign Shorthairs. They have the more wedge-shaped head and long slim body of an oriental type cat, with longer legs, large pointed ears and slanting eyes. Strictly speaking, the Siamese cat belongs in this group, but is placed in a separate class on account of its contrasting point markings. Cats strictly classified as Foreign Shorthairs are available in twelve self-colored, shaded, cameo, tabby and tortie variations, often developed by crossing a Siamese with a domestic shorthaired breed. They make lively and interesting pets that require plenty of exercise. If you have always fancied the snub-nosed expression of a Longhair, or Persian, but could not cope with the grooming, what about an Exotic Shorthair - a cross between Longhairs and American Shorthairs, with the facial expression of a Longhair but the more manageable coat of a shorthair. This is a playful but affectionate cat and great fun. A rich chestnut-colored cat with a short glossy coat is the Havana. Its basically foreign features reveal the Siamese in its breeding, but it manages to have a slightly stockier and more rounded body without losing any of its natural gracefulness. For those looking for something still more out of the ordinary, few cats are as rare as the beautiful Korat or delicate, silky-coated Singapura, with its pale beige fur ticked with brown and cream. Then there is the handsome Russian Blue, with its marvelous silver-blue double coat as sleek as a seal's, or the curly-coated American Wirehair, with its thick, coarse, woolly coat in a wide choice of colors. Many people consider the Abyssinian the loveliest of the shorthaired cats. Again, it combines oriental elegance with a slightly stockier build.

Right: *Some breeds are more active than others. If you choose an Abyssinian, be prepared for an energetic if entertaining companion. Two cats, preferably from the same litter, are good company for each other.*

Below: *Foreign Shorthairs are basically Siamese with no point markings. This Blue occurs naturally, but other varieties, including the Tortie are the result of crossbreeding.*

Left: *Affectionately known as the 'Spottie', the British Spotted Shorthair has a wonderful coat with quite distinct spotted markings. The coat resembles that of a Mackerel Tabby, but broken up into spots rather than stripes. It was first developed in the 19th century from the best-patterned street cats and it quickly became a popular exhibit in the early shows. Today it can be bred in any of the familiar tabby combinations. However, the Silver variety, shown here, and the Brown and the Red are the most popular types.*

Right: *The British Red Spotted Shorthair with its short, thick fur, splendidly displays the tabby-type markings of the 'Spottie' in a rich red against a lighter red background. The large, round eyes are a correspondingly deep orange or copper color. With coloring and markings as handsome as these, this is certainly not a cat to allow out at night and risk being stolen by pelt hunters. As well as being a valuable show cat, the British Spotted is good-natured and intelligent. It will make an attractive and companionable pet for those looking for a strong stocky cat with unusual markings.*

Right: The snowy White Shorthair is much sought after for its purity of coat color despite the fact that the blue-eyed variety has a tendency towards deafness. There is also an orange-eyed White and one with odd eyes - one blue, one orange - which looks very curious and is a side effect of a specific breeding program to produce an orange-eyed White Shorthair with good hearing. The affectionate and intelligent White Shorthair is a well-proportioned, stocky cat, very much at home by the fireside.

Right: The Blue British Shorthair's striking blue coat has made it a firm favorite. The fur is short but dense, producing a plush velvet effect that shows off the blue-gray color to best advantage, while the large, round eyes are copper or orange.

Above: *The stunning Foreign Red Shorthair has a bright red, short, soft coat and green or amber eyes. It was originally the byproduct of a deliberate breeding program intended to produce an all-white cat with the Siamese body shape and distinctive blue eyes. Because back-crossing to pointed Siamese was necessary to achieve the true eye color, some of the kittens in the early White litters were spotted tabbies, solid reds and solid blacks. At first, with interest mainly on the Whites, these were largely ignored, although a few examples were exhibited.*

Right: *The coveted Chestnut Brown Foreign Shorthair is the result of repeatedly breeding Lilac-point Siamese. This program resulted in a number of solid-colored Lilacs with Siamese characteristics – the Foreign Lilac Shorthair shown here, one of today's 12 recognized varieties. This lovely lavender-colored cat with its green eyes is the result of crossing a Lilac-point Siamese with a Havana and it gained full recognition at the same time as the Foreign White in 1977.*

Above: *Foreign Shorthairs are lithe and oriental-looking, with the traditional wedge-shaped head, large pointed ears and attractive slanting almond eyes. There are 12 basic varieties, including this Jet Black with green eyes.*

Right: *The White Foreign Shorthair is not prone to deafness. Foreign Shorthairs are quite different from the British and American Shorthairs.*

Below: *Among the self-colored Oriental Shorthairs, as opposed to the exotic color-pointed class we call Siamese, are a wonderful variety of tabbies, torties and bicolors, all with the familiar slender oriental body type. Other new introductions are shaded, tipped and ticked options, as in this ticked tabby, and an eye-catching cinnamon tabby version. One of the big advantages of a shorthaired cat is that you need not worry so much about keeping it groomed. A shorthair keeps itself reasonably clean and in good condition, unlike a longhaired breed that requires daily attention and if allowed to roam outside would no doubt return full of tangles, twigs and other garden debris. Not surprisingly, since it is far more practical, short hair is much more common among both wild and domestic cats.*

Right: *The elegant oriental physique and short, plush coat of the Foreign Shorthair is perfect for showing off the more unusual or distinctive colors and patterns, such as this Dilute Tortoiseshell. Sometimes called a Blue-Cream, this pretty pastel-shaded pet features a patched blue and cream coat.*

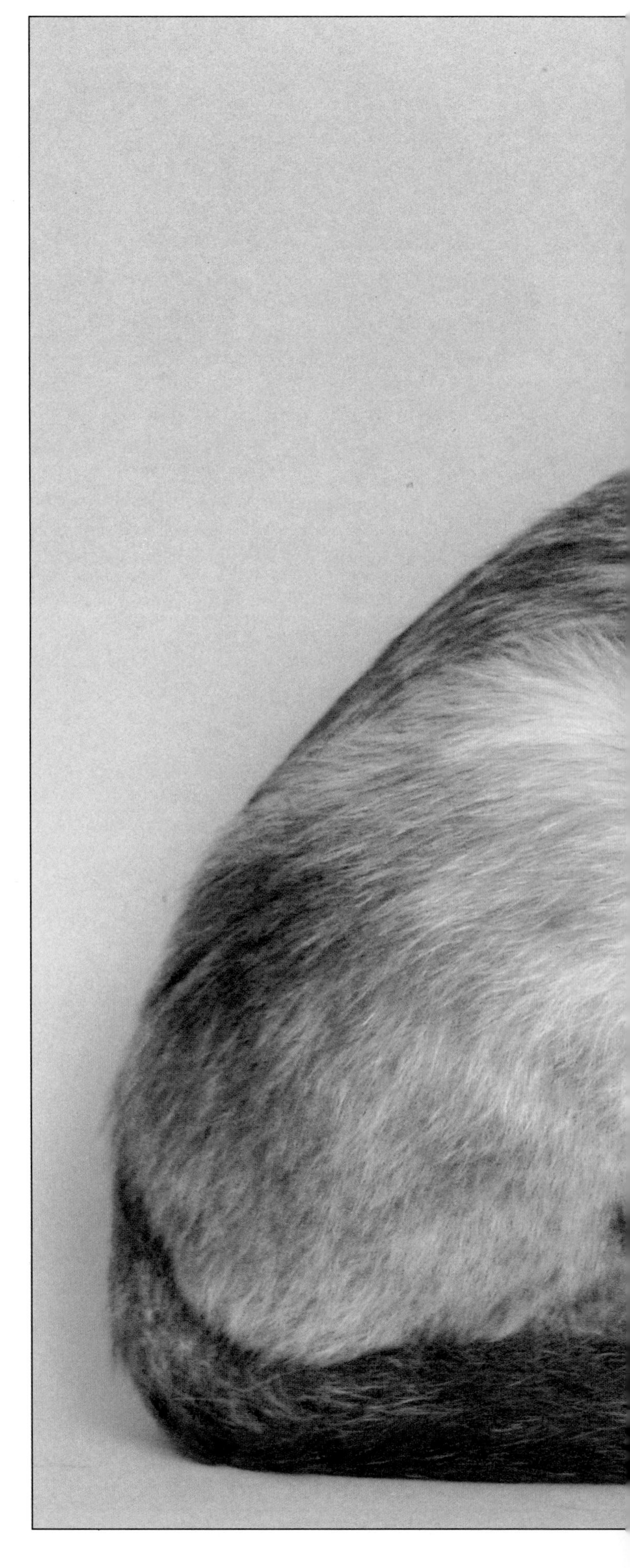

Above: The silky coated Korat is rare even in its native Thailand. A pair of these cats is traditionally presented to Thai brides as a symbol of good luck. Its recognized name originates from the Thai province where it was first developed, and the breed was first imported to the USA from Thailand in 1959, but not officially recognized until 1965. Its body does not have the long slender profile of a typical Oriental, but rather a semi-cobby, muscular physique, with a medium length tail and legs. Apart from its coloring, its face is its most striking feature – an unusual heart-shape with a short nose, large round-tipped ears and large round eyes, which are a brilliant liquid green. Korat kittens are born with yellow or amber eyes that do not turn green until they are two years old. The adult Korat always has silvery blue colored fur with a silver sheen particular to the breed.

Left: *The shorthaired Havana only comes in one variety: a rich chestnut brown with slanted, almond-shaped green eyes. It is the result of a deliberate attempt in the 1950s to breed a cat with the graceful physique of a Siamese, but in an even, solid color. However, if you are interested in showing this attractive and intelligent cat, the US judges prefer to see a slightly shorter, stockier body approaching that of the cob type. The fur should be very glossy and a rich chestnut brown color, like the cigar it is named after. This is a cat that requires plenty of attention, although it will be affectionate to its owner in return.*

Below: *The small, but stocky Singapura is not very often seen in the West, which is a shame as it is a pretty little thing, with large, slanted, almond-shaped eyes of hazel, green or gold, and short, soft, silky fur. As a pet, it has an appealingly quiet nature and enjoys human companionship. Despite the Singapura's delicate appearance and attractive ivory colored coat ticked with brown, in its native Singapore, it is mostly allowed to run wild and is popularly known as the 'Drain Cat' on account of its tendency to shelter in the city's sewer system. A deprived lifestyle has probably accounted for its small stature, yet it is well proportioned, with a finely rounded head and short nose, large pointed ears and small oval paws. Several other color varieties exist in Singapore, but they are yet to be seen in the USA, where the beige/bronze/cream combination is currently bred. The Singapura is not presently recognized for showing in the UK.*

***Left:** The Russian Blue is quite a shy breed and seldom strays far from home, making it a good choice if you want a good-looking, home-loving cat that is a little out of the ordinary. Unlike many other pedigree or unusual cats, the Russian Blue does not demand a great deal of attention or affection. In the past it has also been known as the Archangel Blue, probably relating to the port of Archangel in northern Russia where it originated. It has also been called the Maltese cat. A white version of the Russian Blue was produced in the UK but did not prove very popular among cat owners, so it is quite rare to see one today.*

***Right:** Although elegantly oriental, the short but thick-coated Abyssinian is not as fine-boned as the Siamese. Nevertheless, it is one of the most beautiful breeds of cat, prized for its intelligent expression and lithe physique, as well as the superb plushness of its coat. This copper-colored variety ticked with chocolate is the Sorrel, sometimes called Cinnamon or Russet.*

Below: *Although the standard Abyssinian is a rich gold color ticked with black, other eye-catching shades are possible. These include Chocolate, Lilac, Tortie, Red, Cream and the Silver Sorrel pictured here. This is a relatively new reintroduction and not yet fully recognized by all the associations. Like all Abyssinians, it has an excellent temperament and can be very affectionate towards its owner. These shorthaired cats are easy and quick to groom.*

Siamese and Burmese cats

There is no mistaking the Siamese; it is probably one of the most instantly recognizable cats in the world. It has an ultra-refined oriental profile, startling blue eyes and a pointed elfin face with the mask, ears, legs and tail delicately picked out in a contrasting color. Its voice is unmistakable, too - a piercing, almost human shriek that breeders rather politely call 'vocalizing'. The Siamese can be a noisy and demanding animal if it does not get its own way. Yet its extrovert nature is irresistible, and providing its owner can afford to give it plenty of attention, it will become an affectionate and entertaining pet. The Siamese is probably the most popular of all pedigree breeds, but its origins are not altogether clear. We do know that it was a popular breed in Siam (now called Thailand) as early as the 14th century, and is clearly described in literature of that period as being pale-coated with seal-colored points - the classic Siamese coloring. The history of its introduction to the West is less clear. Siamese cats certainly featured in London's first major organized cat show in 1871, although they were more of a curiosity than a success, being almost the exact opposite of the familiar cobby, shorthaired domestic cat and generally regarded as 'unnatural'. They did not generate much enthusiasm then, but by the late 19th century they were popular enough for standards to be set, although these had to be revised by the start of the 20th century. The early Siamese, for example, had a more rounded head and was prized if it had a kink in the tail - both attributes would be considered a fault in today's show ring. The origins of the kinked tail gave rise to much speculation and various legends grew up to explain it. One declared that the original sacred Siamese temple cats were charged with guarding a priceless vase around which they curled their tails. Another claimed that the royal Siamese princesses kept their rings on the cats' tails, which developed a kink to prevent the rings falling off. Today's lithe Siamese has a long, slim tail, and a wedge-shaped head, with a long nose and large pointed ears, almond-shaped eyes and short, soft, very fine fur. There are four classic colors: Seal-point (cream and brown), Blue-point (pale and slate blue), Chocolate-point (brown on ivory) and Lilac-point (gray-pink markings on a creamy, pink-tinged coat). Other varieties, such as red, cream and tabby or tortie marked points are the result of crossbreeding the Siamese with other breeds, and are described as Colorpoint Shorthairs. One Siamese cross, the beautiful Burmese, is in a class of its own. A perfect combination of both the foreign and the cobbier style of cat, it has an attractive rounded physique with oriental touches, such as high cheekbones and a slant to the eyes. The velvety Brown is considered by many people to be the true Burmese, but there are other colors and patterns, including a Blue and various tortoiseshell colors, all of which have inherited the affectionate, playful nature of the Burmese that makes it such a delightful companion. By crossing the Burmese with an American Shorthair, you get a glossy black Bombay with a really superb coat. A Burmese/ Siamese cross - the Tonkinese - is a more typical foreign build with slim, pointed features and fine almond-shaped eyes.

***Right:** The Platinum Burmese, or Lilac, as it is also known, is a relative newcomer and not recognized by all the cat associations. It has the typically thick plush coat, but is a pinkish gray shade. Because this color variation is comparatively recent, the Platinum Burmese often shows the stockier body shape of the American Burmese.*

***Below:** The pretty Blue-point Siamese has a white coat with a bluish tinge and slaty blue colored points. Its almond shaped eyes are a bright sapphire blue. The Blue-point is one of the four original classic varieties. Although the Siamese is lively and demanding, it is also affectionate and intelligent. It will learn tricks and loves as much attention as you can afford to give it.*

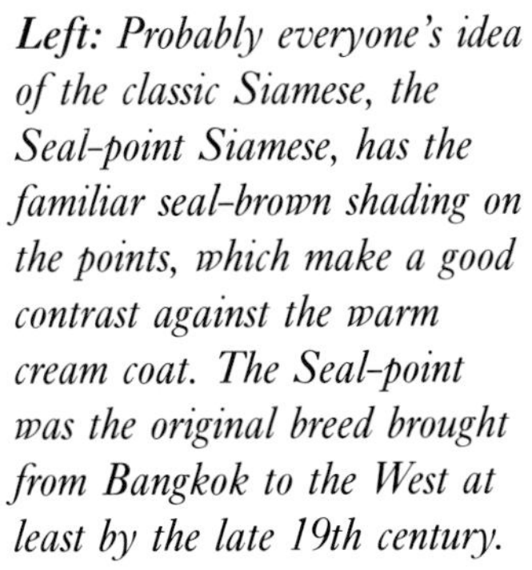

Left: *Probably everyone's idea of the classic Siamese, the Seal-point Siamese, has the familiar seal-brown shading on the points, which make a good contrast against the warm cream coat. The Seal-point was the original breed brought from Bangkok to the West at least by the late 19th century.*

Above: *These days, the point colors come not only in plain shades, but also in the familiar cat coat patterns, such as the Tabby seen here, which is always against a white main coat color. Despite their elegance, Siamese cats enjoy the same activities as other cats, including climbing trees.*

Right: *The Cream-point Siamese is one of the most recent additions to the breed and is very subtly shaded indeed, with warm cream colored points against a white to pale cream background. Siamese kittens are all born white and it is only later that they develop their point colors.*

Left: *Most of the new varieties of Siamese have been developed since the Second World War. The Red-point, pictured here - an apricot shaded cat with reddish-gold points - and the Tortie-points were among the first to be introduced, but many US cat associations still only claim the original four classic colors as being true Siamese. In these instances, the Tortie-points have to be classed as Colorpoint Shorthairs.*

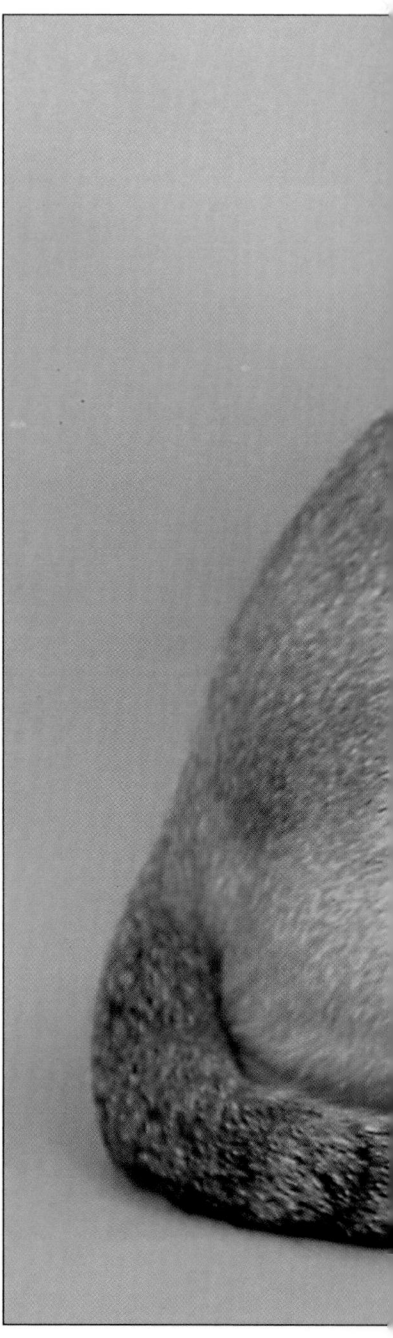

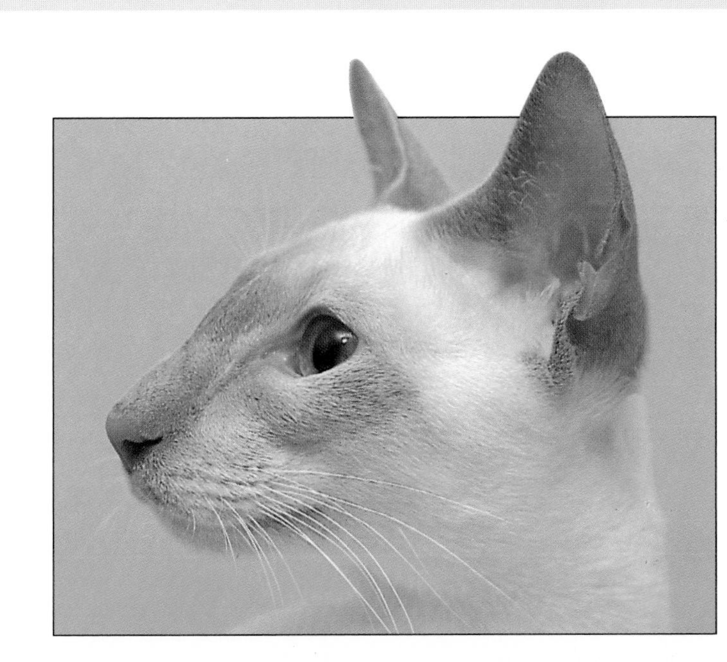

Left: It can be fascinating to watch the points develop: first a thin line appears at the edge of the ears and this gradually spreads to pads, nose and tail. This pigmentation does not reach its full coloring until the cat is virtually a mature adult. The coat color continues to change throughout the cat's adult life, with a tendency to darken after about three years, meaning a show cat can no longer be exhibited successfully. This is a Lilac-point.

Below: One of the new Colorpoint Shorthair varieties bred from Siamese since World War Two is this Chocolate Tabby-point. Tabby-points began to attract interest in the 1960s, although they have been recorded since the beginning of the 20th century. They were officially recognized in 1966 and were soon becoming show champions. They are often referred to as Lynx-points, which is considered more appropriate.

Left: *Most cat organizations recognize the Blue Burmese, with its lovely silvery gray coat. It is perhaps less of a true blue than other breeds, such as the Russian Blue, its sheen having more of a silver tinge. Although it is lively and athletic, the Burmese is surprisingly adaptable and will live quite happily confined to quarters in a city apartment. Character tends to vary - some cats are quieter than others, but none have the rather neurotic temperament of the Siamese and they make excellent house pets for anyone looking for an intelligent and good-natured companion, with the plush good looks of top quality upholstery. Having a short coat, the Burmese's good looks are easily maintained. Despite a natural playfulness, the Burmese never makes a nuisance of itself, even indoors where it will play for hours with some toy or a screwed up ball of paper. If you are interested in breeding Burmese, they are fairly quick to come into heat - maybe as early as seven months old. Litters average about five kittens.*

Below: *Although the Brown Burmese is the original blueprint of the breed, there are nine varieties in total, including the Cream shown here, which is a pure self color with no markings. In all the color variations, the fur is ideally short, smooth and glossy, giving it a wonderfully sleek look that is instantly appealing. It is oriental in appearance, but more round-bodied than the Siamese, with a muscular body, medium length tail and medium-sized ears, slightly rounded at the tips. The head is wedge-shaped but not exaggeratedly so, with high cheekbones and a short nose. The eyes are curiously slanted at the top and rounded at the bottom and are a rich golden yellow color in all the variations. All Burmese are descended from a single dark brown female called Wong Mau, taken to the USA from Rangoon in the 1930s. Attracted by her rich coloring, a breeding program was set up, using a Siamese male as the closest available breed. The all-brown kittens from the resulting litters, were selected and gradually the Burmese breed evolved. Later it was possible to import more cats from Burma to extend the breeding program. Other colors were gradually developed, some outside the USA: the chocolate, champagnes and lilacs, then the reds, creams and tortoiseshells. Not all are recognized in the USA.*

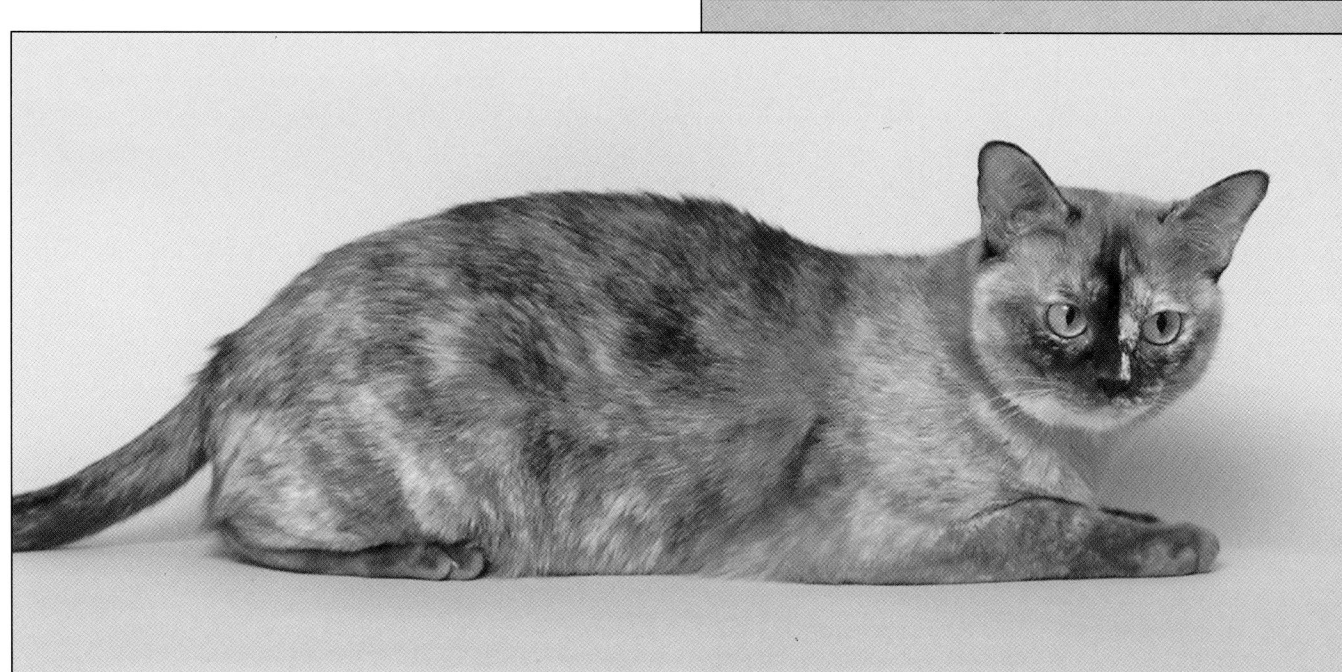

Above: The tortoiseshell variation of the Burmese was achieved by crossbreeding a Burmese with other cats, including a tortie-and-white farm cat. The result of further selective breeding was a Brown Tortie sporting a rich brown coat with red patches, and a Blue Tortie, a mixture of blue-gray and cream. It was decided that blotches, patches and a mingling of shades would be allowed, but in the Burmese, the overall pattern tended to be smaller than in other tortoiseshells. Soon it was agreed to interbreed these two types to improve the stock and extend the color range of the Burmese still further.

Right: The Chocolate Burmese, also commonly referred to as the Champagne, was first bred in North America in the late 1960s and early 1970s, together with the paler Platinum, or Lilac, variety to which it is genetically linked. All the kittens are virtually white when born, so it can be difficult to tell one color from another until they are several weeks old. The Chocolate develops into a pale milk-chocolate color, with slightly darker shading on the head. This contrast often becomes more pronounced as the cat grows older and the tone darkens, much to the chagrin of the breeders who prefer a more subtle graduation. A Chocolate Tortie and a Lilac Tortie have been bred - but not recognized in the USA - giving the Burmese one of the most varied color ranges. The Burmese is quite a long-lived cat, surviving for 16 to 18 years, sometimes even longer. It brings much pleasure to its owners, for it is good-natured, as well as truly handsome.

Below: *The classic Brown Burmese, with its glossy sable brown coat and golden eyes. It has been acknowledged as the primary Burmese since the 1930s. Standards regarding the perfect example of the breed vary around the world. North American shows prefer a much rounder type of cat, whereas the UK likes to see a more foreign-looking wedge-shaped head - not as acute as the Siamese but definitely oriental in style. British judges also prefer the eyes to be more oval in shape. However, everyone is agreed on the coat: it should be short, glossy and very plush, almost like satin.*

Right: *By the mid-1970s, a deliberate breeding program carried out mainly in the UK had produced a self-colored Red Burmese, as shown here. Often the pampered pet or proudly protected showpiece of an apartment dweller, the Burmese is equally at home outdoors. It will enjoy free access to the garden, where it will gleefully romp about - an amusing trait in an adult cat of some dignity. The cat's inborn intelligence, combined with a strong muscular body, makes the Burmese an excellent catcher of rats, mice and other rodents, which it will frequently eat with relish.*

Above: A Burmese crossed with a Black American Shorthair, produced the Bombay, renowned for its exceptional coat, quite unlike that of any other cat. The fur is such a regular color and so close lying that it is said to resemble patent leather. The Bombay's general shape is fairly stocky, medium-sized and muscular, but with surprisingly dainty paws. The rounded head has a short nose and the round, deep copper-colored eyes glow like hot coals. Playful and affectionate, the Bombay is ideal for someone who wants a constant companion, as it will be quite happy to sit on your lap and purr all day, but becomes disgruntled if left alone for any length of time.

Right: Confident and affectionate, the beautiful Tonkinese has an elegant slim body and short, soft fur in a range of subtle brown and silvery shades, with a natural sheen. Its oriental physique is a clue to its exotic origins: the cat is a hybrid of the Siamese and Burmese developed in North America in the 1970s. In fact, this was the first pedigree breed to originate in Canada and has since become popular in the USA, Europe and Australia, although it has not yet been recognized in the UK. The Tonkinese is a lovely blend of both parents: it does have darker shaded points, but these are less of a contrast than in the Siamese, subtly merging into the main body color, which is somewhere between Burmese and Siamese coloring. There are five color varieties but the most common is the so-called Natural Mink - a warm brown with chocolate markings. Equally stunning are the Blue Mink, a blue-gray with slate blue markings; Honey Mink, a ruddy brown with chocolate markings; Champagne Mink, warm beige with pale brown markings; and Platinum Mink, a lovely pale gray with dark gray markings. The Tonkinese is also an attractive combination of body types: the wedge-shaped head has a square muzzle and long nose. The ears are large and round-tipped, the legs long and slim with small oval paws. The almond shaped eyes are a beautiful blue-green in color.

Longhaired cats

Today's exotic cats with their longhaired coats did not reach Europe until the late 16th century. Before that, all domestic types were the shorthair variety. Their true origin is still a bit hazy - are longhaired cats the straight descendants of the shaggy wild cat or did they develop spontaneously in certain parts of the world in response to cold weather conditions? It is now thought that most longhaired cats are mutations of shorthaired types - you sometimes get a longhaired kitten in a litter - that have been isolated, perhaps by being born in a remote region or by deliberate breeding policy. Most of the longhaired cats we recognize today, with their exotic faces, sturdy cobby bodies and thick silky fur are called Longhairs, also known as Persians in some parts of the world. Thanks to a continuous program of development, there are a great many wonderful color variations, including cameos and tortoiseshells, each classified as a separate breed. When its color and general features exactly meet the breed specifications, a pedigree cat can fetch a handsome price. The Longhair's coat is particularly luxurious because it is made up of two layers: a soft, woolly undercoat and the longer, coarser 'guard' hairs which, on a good specimen can be as long as 4.7in(12cm). The coat, the thickset, rounded physique, broad features, short nose and large, round eyes, all combine to convey that marvellous powder puff fullness. There are several groups of Longhair that have been classified separately: Colorpoints, for example, have the contrasting point markings usually associated with the Siamese. Although they are a result of deliberately crossing Longhairs with Siamese, they have retained the stockier physical characteristics and inherited none of the Siamese's slender profile. There is also a new range of colors yet to be fully recognized by the major cat organizations. These colors are generally referred to as New Longhairs and include a Chinchilla Golden and a Lilac-Cream. There are also several known breeds that have long coats but are not included in the Longhair classification. Most have originated in colder countries and their coats are not usually as thick or full as the true Longhairs. Their body shape does not always conform to the round, cobby type either. These cats may be more oriental in build, with slimmer, longer bodies and tails and a more wedge-shaped face. The Balinese is one example - a longhaired mutation from Siamese stock - and the beautiful Birman is another. It has Siamese coloring but a kind of hybrid body shape, being long but muscular, with full cheeks and slightly slanted eyes. The Angora is very slender, too; its coat is long and silky but not as full as the Longhair's. This breed almost disappeared in the shadow of the Longhair's popularity, but is coming back into fashion through direct imports of these cats to the USA from Turkey.

Above: *The eyes of the White Longhair can be orange or blue, or sometimes one of each as here where orange and blue-eyed cats have been interbred.*

Below: *Tabby Longhairs are comparatively rare and this Blue Tabby even more so, since it is not recognized outside the USA. It has an ivory-blue coat with slate markings and copper eyes.*

Right: *Bicolors such as this Red-and-White occur in any recognized solid color mixed with white, the color predominating, except on the underparts. Torties, especially this Dilute Tortoiseshell, or Blue-Cream Longhair tend to have separated patches of color.*

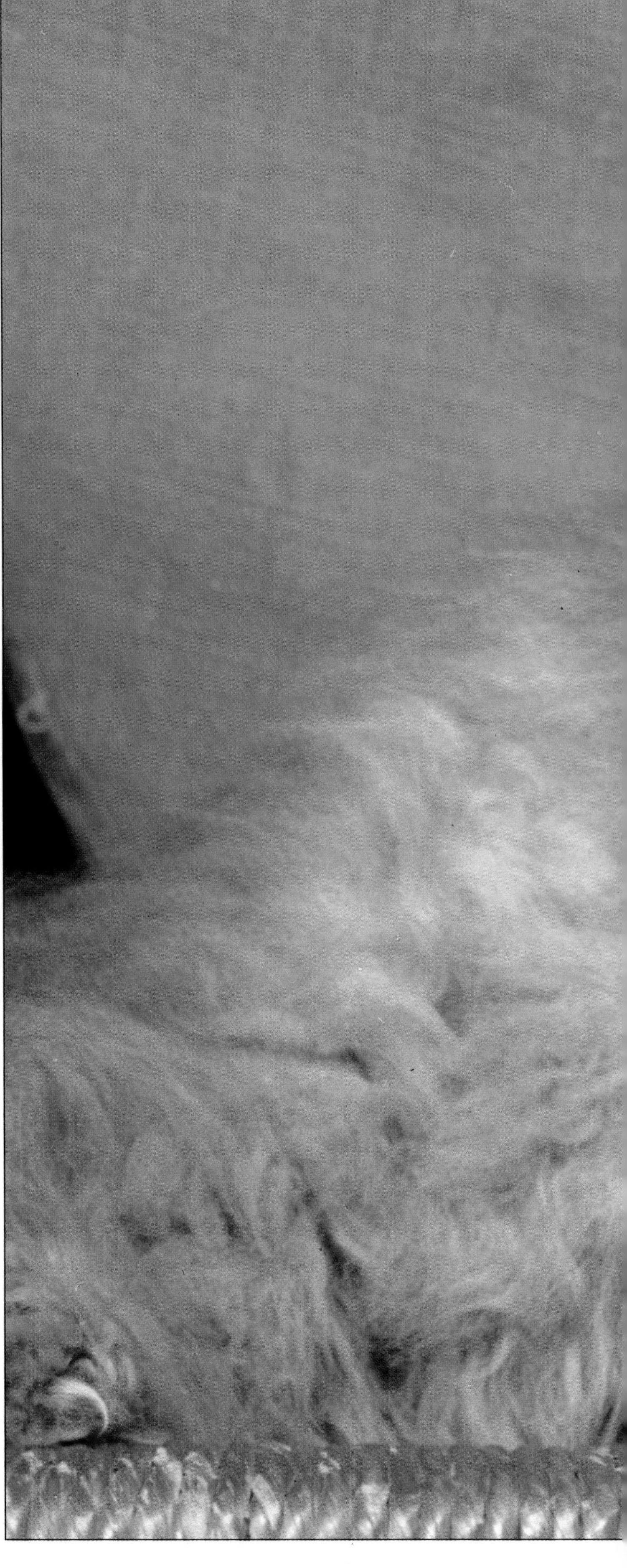

Above: *The White Longhair was the very first longhaired cat to be introduced to Europe, as early as the 16th century. These specimens were more like Angoras, but from the mid-19th century it was possible to breed these with true Longhairs to produce today's White variety. Typical of all Longhairs, the White has a thick coat of silky fur but with a full ruff around its neck, which makes the broad cheeks look even fuller and rounder.*

Right: *Most popular of all the Longhairs (or Persians) is the Blue. Unlike many other breeds of cat, the Blue Longhair really is blue in color - not simply gray or silver - and it can be any shade, although the paler versions are preferred. The coat is thick and silky with a generous ruff, and should be totally self-colored with no markings. One of the earliest varieties, the Blue Longhair was probably the result of crossbreeding a Black and a White Longhair, and originally there was a Gray - probably one of the Blue shades and no longer a classification recognized today. Already by the end of last century, the Blue was one of the most popular Longhairs at the shows. Interestingly, of all the Longhair variations, its body shape is nearest that considered perfect for the breed, and so it is often used in breeding programs to improve the stock of other colors.*

Left: *Once called the Orange, the Red Longhair or Persian was developed in the UK earlier this century. A deep rich red color with no tabby markings is preferred, but this has proved virtually impossible to achieve. Most will have some markings, usually on the face, although these are largely disguised by the denseness and silkiness of the fur. It is quite usual for the kittens to show tabby markings during the first few months of their lives. There is a variety of Red with a squashed-in face called the Peke-faced Longhair.*

Above: *Despite its current popularity in many parts of world, the Cream Longhair was originally bred by accident, the result of mating a Blue and a Red, although it is related to early fawn Angoras. Originally, any potential for showing was ignored and they were neutered and sold off as rather attractive pets called 'Spoiled Oranges'. American breeders decided to develop the variety and produced today's powder-puff cat, which ranges from palest cream to buff. These attractive cats have a delightfully placid nature.*

Left: ***Left:*** *'Bicolor' is the word used to describe a Longhaired cat that combines any self-color with white. Bicolors were once included in the 'Any Other Colors' class, but have now been given a group of their own. Originally, the standards specified that the color patches be symmetrical, but today's judges merely require the patching to be even. Where the color is strong, as with this Black-and-White, the contrast is most striking and a good specimen makes both a handsome pet and potential show champion.*

Left: Both Silver and Golden Longhairs are believed to have been bred out of an early Chinchilla called Silver Lambkin as pale silver varieties were popular at the time. These shades certainly look stunning on a cat with a dense silky coat. Today you can choose from a range of silvers, including Silver Tabbies, Silver Chinchillas and Shaded Silvers, sometimes called Pewters. Silver Tabbies are available in both Classic and Mackerel markings and are a silver gray marked in black, with lovely green or hazel eyes. The Shaded Silver, or Pewter, is particularly beautiful, its thick white coat tipped with black, making it sometimes confused with the Chinchilla, although seen side side by side it is easily identified as being darker. It is the result of crossbreeding a Chinchilla, a Blue and a Black Longhair.

Left: *The Golden Longhair, developed from Chinchillas, is one of the new colors recently introduced as the result of an experimental breeding program. Now breeders are hoping to achieve show recognition, particularly with two gold shades. The Chinchilla Golden is a rich cream color, with pale seal-brown tips and green eyes, while the Shaded Golden has much darker seal-brown tips and is a brown-and-cream version of the Shaded Silver, or Pewter, as it is sometimes called. Other new varieties include a Lilac-Cream and a Chocolate-Tortoiseshell. Its thick, silky coat is a splendid mixture of rich chocolate brown, red and cream patches. All these new varieties have a particularly affectionate yet intelligent nature, which makes them a little livelier than many other Longhairs.*

Right: *Chinchilla Longhairs are the result of various cross-breedings made earlier this century. Their long, silky, snowy white fur is tipped with black on the back, flanks, ears and tail and this produces a superb sparkle to the coat.*

Left: *The Maine Coon's attractive coat is thick and shaggy, rather than long and silky. This hardy cat has been bred from American farm cats and still enjoys sleeping rough. It clearly requires plenty of space and access to outdoors.*

Below: *The Angora is unusual for a longhaired breed, as it has a long, slim body, long tail, slender legs and a pointed face. Its silky fur is not as thick as that of the Longhair. White is traditional, but there are several colors.*

Above: *Unlike most cats, the Turkish Van actually enjoys swimming, diving off rocks and dog-paddling through the water. It has a long, white, silky coat, with a beautiful auburn head, tail and patches. Like the Angora, it has no woolly undercoat to tangle, as happens in other Longhairs.*

Below: *Breeders are beginning to develop Birmans with new colors at the points, such as red, tortoiseshell and tabby, but the only recognized types are the Seal-point and the Blue-point, pictured here, with its slate-blue points against a blue-white coat. Like all Birmans, the Blue-point is not quite as squat-looking as most longhaired varieties. It has the round head, but the face and cheeks are slightly narrower. The cat's large round paws must feature white gloves and the round-tipped ears should be dark like the tail. The eyes are almost round, with a slight oriental slant and are a bright sapphire blue. The Blue-point was a French introduction in the 1920s, although numbers of both the Blue- and Seal-point dwindled drastically after the Second World War and did not really recover until the 1960s. The Birman is the stuff of legends. It is said that the cats were once pure white with yellow eyes and that many centuries ago, 100 of them were kept at the Buddhist temple of Lao-Tsun in Burma. One night, raiders reputedly attacked the temple as the priest knelt in front of the golden, sapphire-eyed statue of the goddess Tsun-Kyan-Kse and killed him. His favorite cat immediately jumped onto the body and as it did so, it received the priest's soul. The cat's fur turned from white to gold, its eyes became sapphire blue like those of the goddess and the feet, mask, tail and legs turned brown, except where they rested on its master. Birmans are also known as the Sacred Cats of Burma, and Tibetan Temple Cats.*

Right: The pretty *Balinese, with its sleek body shape and soft, medium-length coat, is actually a longhaired Siamese, with the same distinctive wedge-shaped head and bright blue eyes. It appeared as a natural mutation in Siamese litters in the USA in the 1950s, and although the coat is neither as long nor as luxuriant as in the Longhair, there is no denying its appeal.*

Curious cats

People who are attracted by the rare or unusual may well seek out a curious-looking pet, and there are certainly some oddities in the cat world. The great majority are the result of some natural mutation at birth, producing exaggerated features or a different fur type. These have attracted the interest of amateur or professional breeders, who have isolated and refined such forms into new breed classifications. Others are natural breeds that are rare simply because they are difficult to breed or come from some remote part of the world and are infrequently seen. There are also some breeds of cat that have been deliberately developed through trial and error or in accordance with a specific breeding program designed to combine certain characteristics of different breeds - perhaps by changing the body shape, length of fur or coloring. Not all these unusual breeds are fully recognized across the world so they cannot be exhibited, but people continue to breed them as a novelty or in the hope that they will be accepted one day. Not only are such cats often expensive, but most also require considerable care if they are to remain healthy and in good condition. Some of the mutations are very strange indeed; perhaps the cat has no tail like the Manx. It sometimes has a rudimentary stump, but the true type has no tail at all. This strange-looking cat - with its stocky body and short, thick fur - has longer legs at the back than the front, making it move rather like a rabbit. At least you can cuddle it; the wrinkly Sphinx, although affectionate, does not like being petted. Mind you, its appearance does not invite you to touch it, being all skin and bone, with huge ears and round copper eyes like some kind of alien. However, if you look carefully, you will see that it is covered in a layer of fine down. The Rex, while not completely hairless, has such fine curly fur that it looks very delicate. In fact, both the Devon and Cornish Rex - two separate breeds - are energetic and playful and enjoy getting up to all kinds of mischief, but they do need some protection against extremes of weather. From cats with no fur or only a very thin coat, to one with such splendid fur that you dare not let it out of your sight for fear of cat thieves. The Egyptian Mau is quite a big muscular cat with a rounded, wedge-shaped head, beautiful almond-shaped green eyes and the most wonderful spotted coat. This rare and friendly breed is probably the result of a deliberate breeding program. The Scottish Fold looks as though it has no ears, but in fact they are folded forward over the head, giving it a most curious expression. The Manx, Sphinx and Scottish Fold originally occurred by chance in litters and were specifically bred to maintain their curious features. The Japanese Bobtail, however, occurs naturally in Japan. Its tail is quite unlike that of any other breed of cat, being short and curled, which makes it look rather like a rabbit's bobtail. Apart from this, it is rather an attractive cat, with a foreign/cob cross body type and a range of colored markings. The Mi-Ke seems to be the most popular of the color varieties; it is black, red and white or tortoiseshell-and-white.

Right: *The stocky Egyptian Mau has a fabulous coat, patterned with elongated spots in four varieties: Silver with dark gray markings; Bronze with dark brown markings; Pewter with gray or brown markings; and the Smoke, which has a thick white undercoat with dark gray tips and jet black spots.*

Below: *The Cornish Rex is the result of a natural mutation that occurred in the 1950s and was developed through a deliberate breeding program. Today it is bred in a wide range of colors, including this Blue Smoke. Unofficially, there is also a blue-eyed variety with Siamese type point markings, dubbed a Si-rex. The Cornish Rex has a slender body, with small oval paws, but the head is the standard wedge shape with large pointed ears and a long nose.*

Below: ***Below:*** *The Cornish Rex is completely different from the Devon Rex genetically, but very similar in appearance, with its short, silky, curly coat. The Rex breed was first recognized in 1967 and is now accepted worldwide. These distinctive Calico Cornish Rexes combine one of the more unusual color patterns – chintz or calico-like patches of tortoiseshell-and-white – with one of the curiosities of the cat world. Both Devon and Cornish Rexes make good pets. They are lively, entertaining and affectionate and do not shed their fur. The Cornish Rex, in particular, is vulnerable to extremes of weather and will need some protection if allowed outdoors. It has no guard hairs: in fact the kittens are often born hairless – a very strange sight.*

Right: *The pixie-faced Devon Rex is a curious little thing and a naturally mischievous creature. Together with the Cornish Rex, it is one of two breeds of curly coated cat. Although it has the typical slender body shape of the foreign type of cat, the head is unique: the enormous pointed ears and wide cheeks dominate, tapering away to a short nose and giving it a cheeky expression. Although the fur is curled, it is very thin and short, sometimes giving it a meager appearance. Although the term 'Rex' comes from rabbits with a similar mutation, an extrovert and affectionate character and its curly coat have often given the Devon Rex the name 'poodle cat'. Except bicolors, all coat colors and patterns are found, including this Silver Red.*

***Left:** The short flat ears of the Scottish Fold are the main distinguishing feature of this very distinctive breed. Its origins can be traced back to a single kitten called Susie that was discovered and registered by a Scottish shepherd called William Ross in 1961.*

***Below:** Famous as the cat without a tail, the Manx originated on the Isle of Man, where it is believed to have been brought from the Far East in the 16th century. Owing to the remoteness of the island, the characteristic remained true. Looking rather like a British Shorthair, except that the hindlegs are longer than the front legs, rather like those of a rabbit, there are two distinct breed variations: the true Manx, or Rumpy, which has a small hollow where the tail should be; and the Stumpy, a cat with a short stump of a rudimentary tail. All the usual shorthair colors and patterns are found in these unique cats.*

***Right:** When a few longhaired kittens appeared in the litters of some Manx cats in the 1960's, it was decided to try and develop them as a separate breed. This program has been successful and the Cymric has been recognized by various cat associations.*

The Ragdoll is a large and unusual cat with the ability to go completely limp and relaxed - like a discarded toy. The origins of the breed remain unclear; we know that it originated in California and is still rarely seen elsewhere, even in the USA. It is said to have White Longhair genes and indeed the coat is thick and long, the body cobby, and the paws large. The cat is believed not to feel pain, which means an injury might pass undetected. Colors include the striking Chocolate-point, pictured left, a Seal-point, a Blue-point and a Lilac-point. The three recognized coat patterns are shown at right: a Bicolor, a Colorpoint and a 'Mitted', with white chest, bib, chin and front paw mittens.

Below: *Very like the Maine Coon to look at, the totally unrelated Norwegian Forest Cat is very rare outside Scandinavia. Its thick, double coat is designed to withstand living outside in the cold and wet. Not surprisingly, it relishes an outdoor life.*

Right: *Forever striving to come up with new varieties, breeders have now introduced the Burmilla - a Burmese crossed with a Chinchilla Longhair. Thus, two attractive breeds with quiet, affectionate natures have produced a good-natured and beautiful cat.*

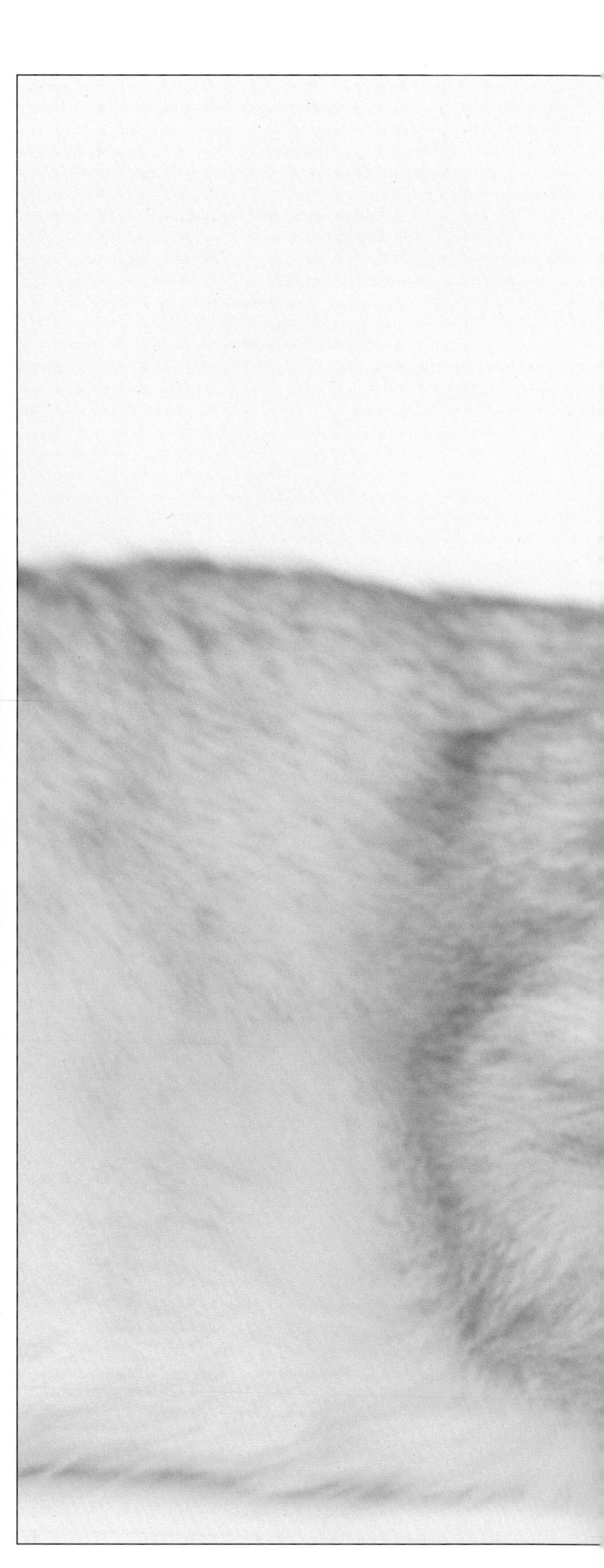

Index

Page numbers in **bold** indicate major references, including accompanying photographs. Page numbers in *italics* indicate captions to other illustrations. Less important text entries are shown in normal type.

Index prepared by
Stuart Craik

Picture credits

The publishers wish to thank Marc Henrie for supplying the majority of the photographs for this book. All are © Marc Henrie.

Other photographs have been supplied by:

C.M. Dixon:
10(BR), 11(B,C)

Images of Africa:
10(BL,TR David Keith Jones), 12(Carla Signorini Jones)

Right: *An elegant Blue-and-white Bicolor Longhair, one of many color varieties bred for the show ring. Perfect examples are difficult to achieve, because the show standard calls for symmetrical patches of color on the head and body, with not more than two thirds of the body colored and not more than one half white. Other permitted color combinations include Black-and-white, Red-and-white, and Cream-and-white.*